Staging Voice

Staging Voice is a unique approach to the aesthetics of voice and its staging in performance.

This study reflects on what it would mean to take opera's decisive attribute—voice—as the foundation of its staged performance. The book thinks of staging through the medium of voice. It is a nuanced exploration, which brings together scholarly and directorial interpretations, and engages in detail with less frequently performed works of major and influential 20th-century artists—Erik Satie, Bertolt Brecht, and Kurt Weill—as well as exposes readers to an innovative experimental work of Evelyn Ficarra and Valerie Whittington. The study is intertwined throughout with the author's staging of the works accessible online.

This book will be of great interest to students and scholars in voice studies, opera, music theatre, musicology, directing, performance studies, practice-based research, theatre, visual art, stage design, and cultural studies.

Michal Grover-Friedlander is Associate Professor of Musicology and head of the Musicology Department at Tel Aviv University. Her first monograph, *Vocal Apparitions: Cinema's Attraction to Opera*, was published by Princeton University Press in 2005. Her second book, *Operatic Afterlives*, was published by Zone Books in 2011. She is artistic founder and director of the experimental opera ensemble *Ta Opera Zuta*.

Routledge Voice Studies

Series editors: Konstantinos Thomaidis and Ben MacPherson

The Routledge Voice Studies series offers a platform for rigorous discussion of voice across disciplines, practices, and areas of interest. This series aims to facilitate the dissemination and cross-fertilisation of voice-related research to effectively generate new knowledge and fresh critical insights on voice, vocality, and voicing.

The Performative Power of Vocality
Virginie Magnat

Beethoven and the Lyric Impulse
Essays on Beethoven Song
Amanda Glauert

Somatic Voices in Performance Research and Beyond
Christina Kapadocha

Owning Our Voices
Vocal Discovery in the Wolfsohn-Hart Tradition
Margaret Pikes and Patrick Campbell

Staging Voice
Michal Grover-Friedlander

https://www.routledge.com/Routledge-Voice-Studies/book-series/RVS
The Routledge Voice Studies series website can be found here: https://routledgetextbooks.com/textbooks/routledgevoicestudies/

Staging Voice

Michal Grover-Friedlander

Routledge
Taylor & Francis Group

LONDON AND NEW YORK

First published 2022
by Routledge
2 Park Square, Milton Park, Abingdon, Oxon OX14 4RN

and by Routledge
605 Third Avenue, New York, NY 10158

Routledge is an imprint of the Taylor & Francis Group, an informa business

© 2022 Michal Grover-Friedlander

British Library Cataloguing-in-Publication Data
A catalogue record for this book is available from the British Library

Library of Congress Cataloging-in-Publication Data
A catalog record has been requested for this book

ISBN: 9781032034270 (hbk)
ISBN: 9781032034287 (pbk)
ISBN: 9781003187257 (ebk)

DOI: 10.4324/9781003187257

Typeset in Times New Roman
by codeMantra

To my lifelong loves Eli, Omer, Elam, Rita and Norman

Contents

Figures

Music examples

Acknowledgements

Staging Voice is not a very long book, but it took me a very long time to find a way for it to acquire form and materialize. Work on and around the book, both on its theory and on the practice the theory reflects on, spanned more than a decade. Thinking of the debt of gratitude I incurred to so many individuals who were crucially involved in the genesis and development of the book, I am still amazed that it turned out to be, ultimately, quite concise. *Staging Voice* is one of those projects that touched continually on my relationship with so many people, that, in truth I wish I could acknowledge everyone in my life over that long and exciting time it came to fruition.

First and foremost and from the bottom of my heart, I thank Eli Friedlander, an admirable stage designer, brilliant reader, wise philosopher, warm, patient, and modest soul mate; my precious beloved and inspiring twins, Elam and Omer, so kind, sensitive, gentle, funny, and gifted, who each in a unique and extraordinary way imbue my life with meaning; my loving, warm, and wonderful parents, Rita and Norman Grover who are infinitely supportive. To Michal Friedlander and Karl-Heinz Steffens, I am grateful for having so much faith in me as a director before I ever directed anything. To the late Hagith Friedlander who always had the best ideas. To David Friedlander, Thom Friedlander, and Coline Faucon for their beautiful designs and materials devised for the operas. I cherish their generous involvement as well as the enthusiastic responses of Saul Friedlander, Orna Kenan, Isabel Gouveia, and Morgan Becerril.

To my friends and colleagues, whose voices and ideas can be found throughout the pages of the book, I extend my utmost gratitude for sharing their intellectual worlds, and being a source of inspiration: Carolyn Abbate, the late Stanley Cavell, Michela Garda, Caroline Bynum, Freddie Rokem, Shizuo Ogino, Arisa Tachi, Jelena Novak, Talia Pecker Berio, and Ruthie Abeliovich.

While I cannot list here everyone who took part in the different productions of *Ta Opera Zuta*, (for that, please refer to footnotes), I would like to acknowledge and express my gratitude to the marvellous and moving singers Doron Schleifer, Yeela Avital, David Feldman and Jonathan Opinya; the inspiring artists, Evelyn Ficarra, Valerie Whittington, Ryo Takenoshita, Daniel Chervinsky, Gony Paz, Ofri Omer, Reenat Caidar Avraham, Nadav Barnea, and Iris Mualem; the wonderful team of singers and artists who were part of a memorable performance of Satie's *Socrate* at Waseda University in Tokyo: Yuki Ohnishi, Mariko Kasahara, Taiki Ikemizu, Yuko Yagishita, Takehiko Kurokawa, and Mao Wada; the dedicated and resourceful producers and assistant-directors Yaniv Baruh, Inbal Gonen, Shira Yasur, and Yoni Garmider; and the generous support of outstanding individuals, Michael Hofmann, Achy Taiber, and Lily Elstein. The first performance of *Ta Opera Zuta* was dedicated to my dearest friend Osnat Avital, whose memory I cherish.

My heartfelt gratitude to friends, students, and colleagues who encouraged, supported, and assisted in so many ways throughout these years: Jeongwon Joe, Gerda Panofsky, Marcus Cheng Chye Tan, Margalit Ziv, Tomer Lev, Zohar Eitan, Dorit Tanay, Ofer Gazit, Stefanie Tcharos, Uri Schreter, Noga Chelouche, Taum Karni, Ira Borsher, Carmina Singers Ensemble, André de Quadros, Common Ground Voices, Yoav Bezaleli, Sharon Zuckerman Weiser, Sophia Ciccone, Kelim Choreography Center, Inbal Shilor Shemesh, Yudit Haviv, Noa Bahar, and Shosh Zeevi.

I am truly grateful to my superb editor over the years, Jim Gibbons, and to the editors at Routledge, Laura Hussey, Ben Macpherson, and Konstantinos Thomaidis for their confidence and unwavering assistance with a somewhat unusual project.

In all honesty, I could not have written anything if it were not for large amounts of coffee, a regular table, and the amazing host of people inhabiting Café Meshulash in Tel Aviv, where every morning my dear Eli and I head out into the world to write.

Introduction
Directing opera, staging voice

Directing opera

1. The singing voice

In many ways, the staging of opera, for all its radical efforts, has not meaningfully taken the singing voice into account. *Staging Voice* reflects on what it would mean to take opera's decisive attribute—voice—as the foundation of its staged performance. The book thinks of staging through the medium of the *voice*. It is an attempt to show a conception of staging that is specifically *operatic* insofar as it thinks everything through the voice's primacy: voice as inflecting meanings, as attuning us to affective mood, as forming character, as providing the impetus or force behind what is enacted and performed, as echoing, even in the design of the stage and the props. Conversely, when voice is staged, one listens differently—in the sense perhaps evoked by Jean-Luc Nancy in *Listening* when he writes that 'to listen is to be straining toward a possible meaning, and consequently one that is not immediately accessible' (Nancy, 2007, p. 6).

To stage the operatic so that it is true to this understanding of the voice's power would be to refract the voice in all the dimensions of signification possessed by the medium: to fashion listening, space, movement and gesture, image and light, enunciations and characters—indeed all aspects comprising a performance—as emanations of the voice. To stage the operatic in the sense I am outlining here would be to bring forth the voice as the original capacity of all performance or that which grounds it, which is fully explored through the staging and performance of the work. Such staging represents a continuous attempt to heighten our awareness of voice and to intensify what singing comes to.

DOI: 10.4324/9781003187257-1

Voice does not serve something outside itself but rather realizes itself in being performed. Performance delivers the voice to what is properly its own. However strange this idea of the voice's overriding importance might sound, it is not new, and it rests upon a central moment in the historical unfolding of singing's significance. *Bel canto*, the term used to capture an aesthetic of voice and singing in Italian opera, signifies opera conceiving itself through its singing voices. It represents the discovery of a world where meaning is entirely established through the singing voice's expressing itself in the performance. *Bel canto* points to the invention of a stage world that is erected by voices: a bewitched world in and of singing, a fantasy of a world made up of nuanced vocal expression and varieties of delivery and execution. The view of staging offered in *Staging Voice* provides a way to intensify, to the extreme, this primacy of the voice, and to have it create a world in—or as—its image.

2. Contemporary opera

There is a wide range of accounts of what opera is and what is essential to it. Some emphasize emotion, exaggeration, intensity; others enchantment, fantasy, or artifice. It is called an art of immersion, a fetishistic enactment of loss, a quest for a lost object; it is viewed as a unity of word and music, a total art or a conjoining of media. Opera is sometimes conceived as possessing unique attributes without which it is not itself. At other times, it is precisely distinguished by the changes it has undergone over its history, its characteristics shaped variously by culture, politics, place, and time. In the present book, I take opera as a medium founded on the primacy of the singing voice. It is a medium that endows voice with a presence through the performer, through what is heard or what is meant, yet at the same time it shows how voice is not reducible to any of these aspects. The singing voice is the soul of opera, what animates it and what it strives to fully express, the means whereby it engenders its manifold manifestations. The attraction exerted by the singing voice is positioned above all the other constituents associated with opera. Accordingly, opera draws us into different modes of listening in general and to the voice in particular. What accounts for opera's specificity, what is referred to as operatic, is not the unique sound of traditional opera's voices. Rather, voice is a power which is given, as it were, occasions to manifest itself, to show its effects. This power's character is mythically expressed in its beginnings, in its origin in the myth of Orpheus, which renegotiates the place of life and of death, of meaningful human existence (Grover-Friedlander, 2014b).

Thus in this book I provide a picture of what staging opera would be or might become first and foremost out of an insistence on expressing what counts as opera, my sense of *what opera is*. But this characterization is made possible in turn by considering what opera has now become and by reflecting on this new condition's relation to what opera once was. It is especially important to be attentive to the medium's vicissitudes when it comes to contemporary works, as these differ from the paradigmatic manifestations of the opera of the past and self-consciously enact that difference: Their attitudes towards traditional opera, drawn mostly from the 19th-century repertoire, are in fact a central theme in these works. Often the traditional forms are criticized as well as used in various ways as springboards for renewed experimentation.

To be sure, one can hold various views about opera's persistence in our world. If one takes opera in the 21st century to exist primarily within a condition of re-enacting a canon of works from the past, then one would also inherit a certain set of elements associated with traditional forms and, with them, the distinctions among words, plot, role, narrative, singing voices, and so on. More often than not, a traditional staging of these works would primarily be rooted in a reading and an interpretation of the verbal text. If one subscribes to this view, such a staging might alter surface elements, for example, by updating the opera (say, transposing its characters and plot to another time and place or by employing new technology). Or a staging might seek to recreate what is known of the work's reception history and produce a version approximating how the opera would have been staged around the time of its composition.

Alternately, one can attend to opera in the 21st century by focusing on newly composed works, many of which seem hardly recognizable as opera as it has come to be known. Indeed, one often encounters such works referred to by the terms *music theatre, composed theatre*, or *post-opera*. Here, that is, one would take the medium of opera to be in a state of radical redefinition and self-critique, revitalizing itself through constant search. In this latter form, opera is viewed as hybrid, influenced by a range of post-dramatic genres—performance art, inter-media, HD live, conceptual art, physical theatre, visual theatre, installation, and the like. In this account, opera that is composed today is genre-blurred, and whatever boundaries it possesses are diffused. In this view of contemporary opera, the medium assimilates characteristics of other manifestations of art music (as in *operatorio*), crosses genres and mingles with pop and jazz (pop opera, jazz opera), assimilates new technologies (brain opera, television opera, interactive opera, visual opera), and so on. A rich field of possibilities has surely opened up for staging in such an environment. There is a way, I claim in *Staging Voice,* to stage what opera has become today so that its latest experiments can be recognized as reflecting an investment in the *voice.*

3. Rethinking the medium

In seeking to explore this understanding of the voice's primacy in staging opera, my book turns to contemporary works, which are critical for any exploration devoted to the staging of the voice. The very transformation undergone by the medium has compelled it to reflect on each and every aspect of the operatic voice and search for ways to express its self-understanding in newly formed voices. Acutely aware of the medium it has inherited, contemporary opera makes this awareness evident in its voices: Their modes of delivery, how they signify, the senses of their materiality made manifest, their ambivalent embodiments, fugitive presence, and more.

With contemporary opera, voice becomes ever more explicitly the subject matter and driving force of the work. Since voice is emblematic of opera, to rethink the medium is first and foremost to re-conceive voice. In traditional opera, voice is sound and technique but also an aesthetics. It is a metaphysics of the voice, an ontology as well as an ideology; it opens for itself a place and relation to culture, to class, to gender and to politics. This means that the revolutionizing of the voice in recent opera includes a challenge to the view that the operatic voice expresses interiority and unified subjectivity for audiences to identify with; it would refuse making the operatic voice into the epitome of beauty through its lyricism, perhaps out of a sense that this perfection depends on ideals that exclude the involvement of technology in its modes of production; it questions the assumption that operatic logic is text- and plot-bound. Contemporary opera might not wish to underscore the virtuosic voice nor its seemingly unique force of projection.

The operatic voice has undergone fundamental transformations on many levels: Traditional sound, technique, and aesthetics have been undone by introducing extended vocal techniques; the position of the singing voice at centre stage has been overturned by post-dramatic theatre and performance art; the ways voices signify and belong to bodily presence has been unsettled by technological remediations; voice's presence, immediacy, and self-identity have been reconfigured in postmodernist contexts.

And yet, for all that, these versions of opera are still opera. The most radical changes in the sound and materiality of opera, in its voices, in the addition of technology, in alternative modes of embodiment or ideology do not leave opera behind as a dead art form from the past. They only widen the scope, deepen and expand the experience of opera. Thus, when I speak of operatic voice, I will use this term to encompass all these developments. Opera goes beyond 19th-century aesthetics and ideology of voice; it lives beyond the repeated hearings of canonical compositions. Opera, having become more interesting and meaningful, now fashions new possibilities for staging its voices.

Staging Voice is an outgrowth of my immersion in, involvement with, and work on opera and music theatre over many years. It presents works that I have interpreted, written about and, most importantly, staged over the last ten years. *Staging Voice* is not only a book of writings about opera or one that gathers my interpretations of specific works: It is an account and an interpretation of the staging of these operas. The works it features are not traditional operas but rather are all drawn from the 20th century, and each in its own way is an outcome of a vehement, at times notorious, reassessment of the medium.

Thus the choice of works. The works considered here are all contemporary. As their titles attest, they are not straightforward operas: They fall variously under rubrics such as 'school opera', 'monody', or 'symphonic drama'. All critically engage with the medium of opera and its voices; all, in other words, acknowledge and respond to the genre itself. Not all these works are well known—small in scale and length, they are thus suitable for a small ensemble. *Staging Voice* is a way to expose and exhibit their critical stances towards opera itself. Dragan Klaic's (1994, p. 74) observation about opera's fringe is pertinent to the works considered in this book:

> here is another world [as opposed to what we find in the large opera houses], a diffused network of small producing organizations where new small-scale opera pieces are developed in modest conditions, with love, care and support that rarely can be found in large houses. In this opera fringe, which has come to existence in just the last few years, new opera or rather new music theater is taken seriously both as music and as spectacle. A limited territory for experimentation has been created.

4. *Staging voice in canonical works*

The ideas put forth in *Staging the Voice* are germane to any opera or music theatre performance, including familiar, frequently staged canonical works. But often, as I have already mentioned, stagings of canonical operas are based on their libretti, with the text governing directorial decisions and the general conception of the performance. In this paradigm of performance, singing is relegated to a means of mere text delivery. That said, certain productions of canonical works have shown the voice being staged. One such wonderful instance is Jean-Pierre Ponnelle's staging of Rossini's *La Cenerentola* (1981). In its sextet, the singers, lit from behind, are transformed into two-dimensional cutouts engaged in shadow play. Not only do the singers exaggerate their pronunciation in order to bring out the form of the six-voice canon, but their movements as well as the overall choreography precisely fit and are correlated with the vocal parts. Staged with the voice in mind, the scene brings out the relationships among the voices as they build the scene's musical crescendo. We are witness to the playful eccentricity of voices. Another example of the staging of voice occurs in Peter Sellars's well-known production of *Don Giovanni* (1990, with Herbert Perry [Leporello] and Eugene Perry [Don Giovanni]). Here the director cast identical twin singers to play the parts of Leporello and Don Giovanni. This choice might come across as sheer gimmickry. But in fact it is a brilliant reinterpretation of the characters' looks in relation to how they sound, a theme that is a key preoccupation of *Don Giovanni*. We find it in the substantial parts of the opera that take place in the dark; in scenes of misrecognition and exchanged identities between Giovanni and Leporello; in the masked ball; and, critically, in Don Giovanni neither possessing any characteristic music of his own nor expressing himself in a contemplative aria, his singing being, more often than not, mirrored in that of the other characters. Sellars has staged the two roles—indeed the two voices—so that they are difficult to distinguish, as if they belonged to a single performer, and in doing so has situated voice as that very plane on which identities are played with.

If we look at what is likely the best-known vocal showpiece—the Queen of the Night's aria 'Der Hölle Rache' from *The Magic Flute*—we can show opposite positions directing a scene of voice in extremis. One approach would draw its conception from an interpretation of the text. Here the Queen's characterization would be taken from the libretto, and her singing would be its illustration. The staging—involving costume, prop, colour scheme, action, lighting, gesture, and so on—reinforces and is integrated into the overall dramatic portrayal of the Queen's rage and vengeance and the depiction of her evil intentions. But one hardly finds a staging of the *voice*. The Queen's psychology serves as an explanation, as it were, justifying the over-the-top singing. The meaning of singing is embedded within and synchronized with the textual interpretation. The scene achieves, so to speak, a quasi-realistic tone, in which high pitch comes across as an expression of wrath, the virtuosic coloratura the unbound force of vengeance.

A radically different approach, though it is also problematic, would be to exclusively feature vocal virtuosity. Contemporary consumption of opera on YouTube has made this a familiar mode. 'Der Hölle Rache', detached from *The Magic Flute*, has been treated as an independent entity. Take the example of the YouTube compilation *40 singers*, which features executions of the staccato passage or of the scene's high note. The same virtuosic passage is consecutively sung by different singers or by the same singer on different occasions. Text and context, made irrelevant, are left out. Voice is staged as competition. Voice is consumed and judged by fans, assessing and celebrating technique and the sound of the voice as such (see Mister Golightly, 2017).

5. *Theoretical framework*

In seeking a theoretical framework for the different productions considered here, I would like to clarify first what this book does *not* do. It aims neither to present a history of productions nor to chart the present state of staging. It does not provide an overview of scholarship on staging opera—an expanding area that includes histories of staging, questions of mediation and technology, the individual styles of specific directors, and accounts of specific stagings. Likewise, the book is not about the process and the collaborative work involved in directing, as is found in rehearsal studies or artistic based research. The book does not present a theoretical framework in which the works and their interpretations might serve as illustrations. Neither does it suggest a theory nor develop a vocabulary for staging opera, though it points in these directions and may help to advance such undertakings.

I am hoping that the examples the book works through, the ways it brings together research and actual stagings, as well as its original stagings and unique approach to staging *voice* will prove inspirational. The book is intended for academics and artists alike. As far as I know, it is the first book ever written on directing from the perspective of a musicologist who is also a director. The modes of staging voice outlined below are of value to reflection on other operas, both in the abstract and in performing and directing them. The book will, I hope, be valuable to director, performer, and scholar, and will add to our experience of performances of voice.

I am hesitant as to how to position and frame this book theoretically. It deals with interpretations of operas, so in that sense it is situated within Opera Studies. The specific works I discuss, however, are often not considered opera. Moreover, I know of no precedents in which a musicologist directs. Musicologists specializing in opera have often served as dramaturgs (Carolyn Abbate, David Levin, and Jelena Novak, to name a few) or have developed interpretations of other directors' work (the list is long: Emanuele Senici, Melina Esse, Nina Eidsheim). Studies pairing scholarship with directing are more frequently found outside musicology, in Theatre and Performance Studies (Nicholas Till, David Roesner). Often the methodologies derive from or are associated with practice and/as/based research and their offshoots.

Calling for a voice-centred approach to staging, *Staging Voice* thus differs from a recent account of operatic staging (see below: David J. Levin's *Unsettling Opera*) and indeed from any other current scholarly approach to opera production. It offers a way to think about practice-based research in which scholarship and performance mutually reinforce each other. And it speaks to the recent emergence of Voice Studies as a sub-discipline by proposing an approach to staging voice that informs and is itself informed by contemporary experimental practice. Scholarship in each of these fields is vast and constantly expanding. In what follows I have engaged with some of the scholarship and explored how it bears on, and differs from, my approach.

6. Scholarship on staging opera

Staging Voice adds a new perspective to an emerging field devoted to the study of staging, initiated in the first decade of the 21st century by two monographs on staging opera: Roger Parker's *Remaking the Song* (2006) and David Levin's *Unsettling Opera* (2007). For Parker, staging is part of opera's mutating text, and for Levin it provides the opportunity to mount internal criticism of the medium. Parker's interest in *Remaking the Song* is in the ways the opera repertory has been transformed from within. Operas are not unalterably set and closed texts. The 'work concept' has always been problematic with regard to the genre of opera, not only because many composers have produced numerous versions and revisions of their operas, but also because of the role of the performers in reviving and transforming the work. Parker claims that works are repeatedly performed and have remained alive for so long because of performers. *They* transform works, create new ways to listen to them, mount new interpretations, and establish novel associations. Staging is thus one aspect of this sort of transformation which characterizes the internal life of operas over time. But staging, Parker argues, does not go far enough if it shies away from altering the music as well. Opera is inherently mutable, and staging is one of its changeable constituents.

In *Unsettling Opera*, Levin seeks to arrive at criteria for evaluating and assessing productions. His aim is to provide a vocabulary and a methodology for charting the meanings opened up specifically by staging. He devises a vocabulary and a classification for staging, and develops categories for it as well. Such terminology serves in part to overcome the risk of falling back on a simplistic division separating conventional from experimental stagings. More importantly for Levin, this framework not only enables an evaluation of productions in terms of work and score but also allows us to focus on how staging alters the opera being staged and shapes our understanding: 'Any production can unsettle opinions that had become settled' (Levin, 2007, p. xvii). Levin explores canonical works reconceived via particular stagings and draws out a sense of how such stagings reveal something about the work itself and about opera as such. Opera is suffused with contradictions and tensions that traditional, fixed staging, consciously or not, strives to mask, thus hiding what is essential to the genre. A significant production finds ways to alert us to opera's excesses, contradictions, and incongruities; it illuminates the piece and opens it up to further possible interpretations. Opera is flexible enough, Levin claims, to encompass the most extreme and radical recasting achieved via staging. And, conversely, staging reveals that opera itself is something fundamentally unsettled, unruly, in excess of itself.

The observations made in David Roesner's *Musicality in Theatre: Music as Model, Method and Metaphor in Theatre-Making* (2014), in which music is what initiates staging, are closer to my ideas about staging voice than those advocated by Parker or Levin, even though Roesner does not deal with opera. Roesner explors cases where theatre works through musical analogies and musical metaphors, where the music's techniques, abstractness, independence from language, and non-representative character are adopted as a model (Roesner, 2014, p. 10). He deals with what he calls the musicality of theatre: with music's aesthetic, formal and abstract attributes and its social, ideological, cultural, and embodied dimensions. I find that his notions of musicality and 'composed theatre' bear resemblance to how I view voice's place and importance in staging opera. What is more, staging voice and staging music frequently go together and at times are hard to tell apart.

Nicholas Till, writing about his staging of Stefano Gervasoni's music theatre piece *Pas si*, is even closer to the ambitions of *Staging Voice* in that he writes on the staging he himself conducted and derives the concept of staging from the piece's critical stance towards opera, as embedded in the music itself. Till explains: 'I am excited by Gervasoni's music, and eager to find out how his aesthetic translates into the language of a "post-operatic" music theatre that accepts the constituents of opera but challenges the dramaturgical and ideological assumptions underpinning its forms' (Till, 2013, p. 223). The score and the singers' process of learning the music together suggest the approach he should take regarding staging and theatricality; the audible dimension determines the form and the concept.

7. How to write about staging

What do we write about when we write about staging? What do we interpret? Where does such writing belong? Is it part of the discipline of Performance Studies, or of Performance Analysis, Practice-led Research, Practice-based Research? The theoretical questions grappled within this book are central to contemporary attempts to come to terms with the slippery character of performance. What you write about when you write about staging, and how to write about staging, are matters situated within a larger debate: Whether the unique, non-repeatable, present, ephemeral moment of performance reveals something that is unavailable to the work and its interpretation. The field of Performance Analysis emerged with the goal of developing ways to write about fleeting, unique occurrences revealed only in the execution and experience of a performance, which take the form of rifts that could only have occurred on a particular stage with these specific performers at this given time, and only as the result of a specific audience being present. Performance Analysis's aim is to focus on the ephemeral, concentrating on the sensorial material event of the performance's occasion as a critical event, as a moment of presence, rather than analysing the signifying systems of the work of art, language and the like (Risi, 2006).

Peggy Phelan has voiced one of the more extreme positions arguing for the impossibility of writing about performance:

> Performance cannot be saved, recorded, documented, or otherwise participate in the circulation of representations of representations: once it does so, it becomes something other than performance. To the degree that performance attempts to enter the economy of reproduction it betrays and lessens the promise of its own ontology. Performance's being [...] becomes itself through disappearance.

> (Phelan, 1993, p. 146)

Because the performance leaves no trace, writing about it necessarily cancels the 'tracelessness' inaugurated by this performative promise itself.

This position has been revised from within various theoretical approaches surrounding performance art, for example by Erika Fischer-Lichte, who claims that the failure of the documentary object and of writing about performance can itself be conceived as productive: 'Dabei ist es gerade die reflektierte Spannung zwischen ihrer Flüchtigkeit und den unablässigen Versuchen, sie mit Video, Film, Photographie, Beschreibungen zu dokumentieren, die auf ihre Ephemeralität und Einmaligkeit unmißverständlich hinweist' ['It is precisely the tension between the fleetingness of performance and the constant attempts to document it on video, films, photographs or descriptions which highlights its unmistakable ephemeral and unique character'] (Fischer-Lichte, 2004). Schneider states that 'performance remains, but remains differently—appears, but appears differently' (Schneider, 2001, p. 101). That is, the performance does not only imply the presence of the body, it is not only a bodily event; what is derived from a performance once it is over also acquires a sense of presence, albeit a different presence.

These discussions have given rise to a series of oppositions: Abbate's distinction between gnostic and drastic; Gumbrecht's presence and meaning cultures; Goebbler's absence vs. presence; Kramer's performance and score or work; and several others. 'What does it mean to write about performed music?' asks Carolyn Abbate in her classic article 'Music: Drastic or Gnostic?' (2004). The passionate discussion that arose in the wake of this essay's publication was directed mainly towards questioning the object of musicological research and the modes of writing about it: Is performance the ineffable 'true' object of musicology? If so, are the interpretative discourses employed in the discipline suitable? Are they relevant?

While Theatre and Performance Studies have opened themselves to new domains such as Performance Analysis, Rehearsal Studies, and Research-as/led-Practice, the challenge is still felt within musicology (see Cook, 2013; Cook and Pettengill, 2013). Lawrence Kramer and Karol Berger responded to Abbate's challenge by arguing that the dichotomy she presents is extreme and misleading. There is a middle ground between 'drastic' and 'gnostic,' embodied knowledge and hermeneutics. Kramer (2011) thus offers to reconcile the opposing claims by arguing that a music work is quite unlike any other art form in the particular affinity between the work's dimensions and its performance:

> musical performances become eventful through the grounds they give—that they invent, discover, fantasize, imagine—for

apprehending meanings that will eventually evolve beyond them. [...] The performance of a score is an invitation to the performance of an understanding. It is an interpretation that wants to be met by another interpretation in a new medium.

(Kramer, 2011, p. 277)

If we read Abbate's essay carefully we realize that she herself argues for this position, as the essay dismantles the opposition it has established:

If speaking of live performances and thus embracing classical music as drastic means dissecting the gnostic attitude, this is not to dismiss hermeneutics or formalism but rather to say that a great deal remains to be thought about performance, which, with infrequent exceptions, is inaudible to both in practice.

(Abbate, 2004, p. 51)

How to write about staging is part of the larger issue of writing and documenting performance. Indeed, what staging could be, how it could be done, and how to testify about it are questions that have been asked more frequently outside of musicology and posed not in relation to staging opera. More often than not, musicologists interpret existing performances and do not write about how to realize staging. I wish not to further summarize the massive scholarship devoted to the nature of performance but rather to simply offer a reminder of the in-between, ambiguous nature of staging within the context of performed music. Staging—indeed, like voice—falls in between or on both sides of numerous oppositions. Staging is both drastic and gnostic yet is not quite either; it is at once a performance and a form of its documentation; it falls under both presence and meaning cultures. It occupies a space between oppositions, situated between notions such as meaning, hermeneutics, and abstractness on one side and those of presence, eventness, and materiality on the other.

8. Voice Studies

I locate the unique and meaningful contribution of *Staging Voice* not in some effort to expand upon existing theories about performance but in offering an approach towards an aesthetics of a voice in performance. Over the past few decades, different disciplines have devoted particular attention to the notion of the voice and its character in the constitution of their specific field of inquiry. The auditory or acoustic turn, and more recently the 'voice turn' (as it is often referred to), have occurred in the humanities, the social sciences, the fine arts, and the natural sciences (Kane, 2015). Voice has become the preeminent object of disciplinary and interdisciplinary interest, and each field of inquiry has developed its own take. Voice is viewed as a condition of sociability, at work in the formation of the law, as an essential component of subjectivity (in philosophy, psychoanalysis) and as expressing agency (political science), as well as standing for the 'body' of language or materiality of meaning (cultural and performance studies). Voice has been examined in several scientific fields. For example, empirical studies of the singing voice, though still in their infancy, have shown that listeners' emotions align themselves with specific expressions of singing. Determinate acoustic and performative attributes of the singing voice such as vibrato, dynamics, and micropauses between syllables are perceived as expressions of specific emotions (Coutinho, Scherer, and Dibben, 2014). Voice is central to theories of power, communication, media, psychology, natural science, and aesthetics. Indeed, the expansion of research on the voice has culminated in the formation of the field of Voice Studies.

Since 2014, several published collections exploring the voice in relation to music have shared a pluralistic and multidisciplinary approach. Walter Bernhart and Lawrence Kramer's *On Voice* (2014) demonstrates, as do several other recent volumes, the plurality of voice. In his introduction, Kramer elaborates on the intrinsic multiplicity of the voice. Many things are considered voice, and different accounts do not speak of the same voice. It would be impossible to offer a theory of voice, as voice is unstable and plural. Kramer instead puts forth what he calls the 'observation' of voices:

> *Observed* in every sense of the word: noticed, heeded, acknowledged, descried. At its most acute, such observation can take the place of theory. Doing anything more than that (but it's already a lot) would reduce the plurality of voice to an allegory of voice. Understanding voice does not *begin* with the observation of voices; it *is* the observation of voices.
>
> (Kramer, 2014, p. xii)

On Voice focuses on the musical varieties of the topic and returns voice to a consideration of the relationship between words and music. What is most relevant to my account in Kramer's position is his call to explore the heightened voice, such as the voices of opera (Kramer, 2014, esp. x). I share the conviction that opera has a privileged position as an art form centring on the voice (Grover-Friedlander, 2014b).

Martha Feldman's (2015b) introduction to the JAMS colloquy 'Why Voice Now' encapsulates the current state of affairs:

> Nowadays, we might say, voice is 3D. Not just fully embodied, it transcends the conventional body to reveal what is most intimate and nuanced in nonconforming bodies, post-human bodies, even holographic bodies, such that the boundaries of the voice are themselves without evident limit. More material and technological [...] Voice is nothing if not boundless, furtive, and migratory [...] For clearly when we say 'voice' we are using shorthand for a dizzying multitude of phenomena and interests.
>
> (Feldman, 2015b, pp. 656–7)

Feldman outlines notions shared by the writers included in the collection: Voice is not unitary but is material, embodied, relational; it is intermediary; it is an in-between notion; it operates at or on borders, is concerned with alterity and difference; it is most characteristic when it sounds.

Indeed, the importance of theories of the voice's materiality cannot be stressed enough. In this context, the writings of Steven Connor, specifically his notion of the vocalic body, has been crucial for any conception of voice, especially any conception that would fully grasp the performativity of the voice and notions of its presence:

> Voices are produced by bodies: but can also themselves produce bodies. The vocalic body is the idea—which can take the form of dream, fantasy, ideal, theological doctrine or hallucination—of a surrogate or secondary body, a projection of a new way of having or being a body, formed and sustained out of the autonomous operations of the voice.
>
> (Connor, 2000, p. 35)

Konstantinos Thomaidis investigates somatic approaches to voice, foregrounding sensation and materiality. These somatic approaches are developed for use in pedagogy as well as for working out new research methodologies. Through the praxis of vocality he explores vocal habits and default patterns (see, for example, Thomaidis, 2021), devising methods for exploring key moments in the construction of one's own voice, a process he terms 'vocal autobiography'. Vocal autobiography not only reveals voice's multiplicity and polyvocality but also refigures our very sense of what the self in autobiography is (Thomaidis, 2020). Ben Macpherson develops the notion of 'somaesthetic vocality'... [which] consider[s] the role of the body in the experience of vocal practice' both for the speaker/singer and the listener (Macpherson, 2021, p. 214). Moreover, the visceral quality of the voice is evident in musical notation, that is, it manifests visually regardless of musical style or historical period (Macpherson, 2015).

In 2019, Martha Feldman and Judith Zeitlin co-edited *The Voice as Something More: Essays toward Materiality*, a response to Mladen Dolar's seminal *A Voice and Nothing More*. The collection interrogates a variety of subjects, particularly self and other, language, grain, technology, music, and race (Feldman and Zeitlin, 2019, p. 4). The editors aimed, in their words,

> to challenge certain commonplaces in thinking about voice. Each contribution in its own way also grapples with the materiality of the voice by keeping concrete, contextualized voices in the foreground, rather than allowing voice as an object of analysis to fade into pure metaphor or figurative generalization.
> (Feldman and Zeitlin, 2019, p. 18)

Alongside these collections is the *Oxford Handbook of Voice Studies*, co-edited by Eidsheim and Katherine Meizel, which views voice as partaking in all the senses and to be crucial to identity constructions. In the introduction, the editors stress the significance of an interdisciplinarity of approaches for dealing with voice and the importance of knowing, acknowledging and engaging different approaches. Eidsheim's books *Sensing Sound: Singing and Listening as Vibrational Practice* (2015) and *The Race of Sound: Listening, Timbre, and Vocality in African American Music* (2019) are important precursors to the Oxford collection. Eidsheim argues we are always 'hearing one's voice through the ears of others'; voice is always culturally conditioned. We 'reduce [sound, voice] through naming' according to preconceived expectations of what the sound should be and what sound is like, particularly when it comes to timbre, and especially in relation to gender, ethnicity, and race. Eidsheim views sound as vibration. She argues against voice as a static and essentialist notion and in favour of a 'principle of vibration'. Aural, listening voices are all multi-sensorial; they are relational, events of the practice and experience of vibration; voice is material and transferable energy (Eidsheim, 2015). Voice forms a multisensory phenomenon, a vibrational practice. She directs the focus away from works and artists and towards performers and audiences, to those who vocalize and those who engage in the act of listening. Her examples are drawn from experimental vocal music. She analyses underwater opera and various experimental vocal practices. She also considers the assumptions underlying voice pedagogies and technologically created voices (such as the synthetic vocaloid). Her aim is to widen the experience and notion of what listening and vocalizing entail, what goes into productions of sound, and how such productions are determined by reception and prior judgement. Not only listening but vocalizing, too, depends on the conditions of listening and on specific listeners. Eidsheim undermines widely held assumptions and convictions: '[the human] voice is not singular; it is collective'; 'voice is not innate; it is cultural'; 'voice's source is not the singer; it is the listener'.[1] As distinct from a previous surge of scholarship on voice in the 1990s, Feldman and Eidsheim and many of the writers in their respective collections emphasize historical, cultural, and identity politics. By contrast the scholarship of the 1990s, more often than not, had written of the metaphysics and the ontology of voice—an emphasis still found in Kramer's views and, to some extent, in my notion of staging voice.

More relevant to my work than the two collections just mentioned is *Voice Studies: Critical Approaches to Process, Performance and Experience* (2015), co-edited by Konstantinos Thomaidis and Ben Macpherson. Comprising essays on voice in performance, the collection offers an overview of theatre's and performance's relation to theories and performances of voice. Here, too, plurality, in-betweenness, interdisciplinarity form the approaches to voice. The book's essays explore transitions, passages, and transformations made possible through voice as theorized in various discourses and methodologies. Voice lies in between the practical and exegetic; it is both method and tool. It occupies a zone, for instance, between body and language (Dolar, 2006); it is neither linguistic, nor timbral, nor tonal (Roland Barthes); it is both permanent and transitional, is neither an object nor belongs to a subject (Cavarero, 2005); it is simultaneously a person's, a character's, and a musical instrument (Frith, 2008); it is at once present and disembodied (Neumark, Gibson and van Leeuwen, 2010).

Ben Macpherson develops the notion of voice as a reciprocal process, existing as 'a sonic in-between.... [V]oice [i]s an experience shared by both speaker/singer and listener' (Macpherson, 2021, p. 220), and this experience is embodied, somatic, corporeal. 'Voice, then, is a plurality—and the aural "in-between" is the junction point for multiple encodings of experience to be negotiated and understood' (Thomaidis and Macpherson, 2015, p. 4). These experiences are cultural, neurobiological, and sensational. Indeed, for Macpherson, in-betweenness lies in 'a tripartite process of embodied experience ... flowing from the vocalizer, through the in-between of space, to the corporeal listener'

(Macpherson, 2021, p. 223). Katherine Meizel coins the term multivocality to signify vocal ways of being through voice. Singers navigate the in-betweens and border crossings of their identities in their voices (Meizel, 2020). Norie Neumark listening to media and digital arts writes about voice as paradoxically lying in-between embodiment, alterity, and signification (Neumark, Gibson and van Leeuwen, 2010).

Interrogating the performativity of voice has been a central feature of much contemporary experimental theatre. Herbert Blau has described how he 'wanted a way [...] to exercise the voice that would be at every moment inseparable from the art of acting, something of a *performance itself*' (Blau, 2002, p. 125, emphasis added). Doris Kolesch has given an account of the exploration of voice in theatre by artists such as Christoph Marthaler, Heiner Goebbels, Frank Castorf, and Einar Schleef, each of whom, in different ways, have shaped the performance through voice (Kolesch, 2013, p. 107). These scholars have described a phenomenon for which 'the voice [constitutes] a performative phenomenon par excellence ... [New theatre] produc[es] acoustic phenomena with their own intrinsic value' (Kolesch, 2013, p. 109).

Finally, Hans Ulrich Gumbrecht brings together materiality and significance when he writes about the role of the performed voice in staging opera; indeed, he privileges opera and its singing voices in his matrix of presence and meaning cultures. In meaning culture, the world is interpreted by identifying deep-seated meanings underneath appearances, and knowledge is produced through the exercise of thought. In presence culture, the principal self-reference is the body. Staging of opera works on, through and with both sorts of cultures. Gumbrecht identifies 'vocal remnants'—a force in the act of singing that is material and tangible (Gumbrecht, 2005). These remains, or the force of the voice, manifest themselves as moments of intensity that elude meaning. But in fact these 'presence effects' result from an immersion in meaning culture, which is founded on hermeneutics. For Gumbrecht, opera is that medium that thrives on the oscillation and tension between meaning and perception and their two forms of production: 'meaning' and 'presence'.

9. *Relation to my earlier work*

In many respects, *Staging Voice* extends the themes raised in my previous books. The earlier themes of my reflections on opera are here brought to bear on my understanding of the staging of the voice. One such theme concerns the voice's transformations when it is translated into a different medium. In my first book, *Vocal Apparitions:*

The Attraction of Cinema to Opera (2005), I was concerned with the transformation of the operatic voice in the transition from opera to cinema for the sake of studying the medium of opera from an external standpoint. In my writing about opera and cinema, I emphasize what specifically occurs when what is aesthetically essential about one medium is transposed into the aesthetic field of the other. It is not the case that opera and film lose what is characteristic to each of them in this transformation. Instead, the transformation points to the specificity of each medium, in ways that consideration of opera or of film on their own respective terms could not reveal. Thinking about one medium through the other uncovers something about their relation in a manner available neither in the abstract nor by way of theoretical accounts alone. Cinema, at times, can be more operatic than opera itself, capturing something essential that escapes opera's self-understanding. In the idea of the refraction of one medium in another, we find new openings for interpretation and criticism. Through another medium, the fundamental meaning of voice and singing in opera is made uncanny or strange and shown to be inherent to the medium as such.

A related theme central to my previous books that will be encountered in almost every chapter of this book is the affinity between voice and death. Voice makes its power evident in relating to this constitutive limit of existence. My second book, *Operatic Afterlives* (2011), dealt with liminal cases of operatic singing through its interpretation of images of singing and of the voice after death. Voice is figured as the capacity to cross the threshold separating the living from the dead, to transform the one into the other, as a power to revive the world. I term this conception *afterlives of voice*. Redrawing the boundaries of mortality through the notion of the afterlife of singing makes manifest a sphere of singing with its own distinct qualities and conjoined meanings. This sphere of singing reformulates what operatic singing involves: Death, the limit zone, is revisited and renegotiated, and there emerges a new extremity, a beyond of death, around which the presence and self-awareness of singing is reconfigured. It exemplifies a fantasy of opera, namely, its power to overturn mortality. Afterlives of voice are cases when a passage between the worlds of the living and the dead, what opera has always wished for, is granted. The ways afterlife figures in the special cases dealt with in *Operatic Afterlives* become ways I think about staging voices. Different possibilities for staging open up: Options exploring modalities of disembodiment and re-embodiment, of multiple voices, multiple bodies, of merging, mismatched and odd timbres, of voices of the inanimate and of objects. The voice may disentangle itself from what envelops it and become its own being.

In my current book on staging I further test the idea, central to my earlier work, that the singing voice carries the weight of the work. Singing is an unbound reverberation of modes of meaning. I place the idea of voice together with its realization in performance and show how thinking and listening to the singing voice can be enacted in the actual, concretely perceived world of performance. I argue that such singing calls for unique conceptions for its staging. While I think of the idea of staging voice as bearing on different domains of performance, such as the staging of theatrical voices, it is nevertheless important to also bring out the peculiarities of the operatic voice—its materiality and disembodiment, its imaginary, auditory qualities—and the way these voices call for distinctive staging.

Staging voice

1. Modes of staging voice

A modest monograph focusing on a few works cannot do justice to the potential inherent in staging voice. So before I go into my own work, I will offer an initial classification, sketching a few possible modes of staging voice, some of which feature in my work. They are not meant to codify my directorial choices, and I will not refer to them in the sections devoted to staging in the chapters themselves (though they will be mentioned in the short introductions that I place before each chapter to provide orientation). My intention in this initial classification is to point to the huge potential of staging voice and to abstract general principles that may be useful for other directors. These possibilities, needless to say, are not exhaustive and do not cover the full potential of an aesthetics of staging grounded in the voice.

The first mode of staging voice can be dubbed *all ears*. It is found in performances that focus predominantly on the sense of hearing, for instance, in performances or other kinds of events occurring in the dark. These events are specifically designed to be aural experiences, interrogating visuality and tactility by means of the aural. At times, the performance is assisted via headphones, so that voices and sounds are positioned directly 'in' the ear (Kendrick, 2017).[2] An example is *War Music* (1998) by Sound&Fury, in which a play took place in utter darkness and each and every aural detail was heightened, the environment being entirely sonic. Any sense of time and the movement of voices through space was enhanced by the sound design, the use of sound effects, and various vocal textures (Espiner and Cook, 2017).

The second mode one may term *composed staging*. It is found in contemporary opera for which staging is inseparable from composing. Writing for the voice and staging take part in the same process. Staging is thus embedded in compositional ideas and, at the level of conception, voice has already been staged. This mode is often operative when technology is involved in the work and mediates the singing voice (Novak, 2015, p. 150). It is common in works that employ live performance and digital technology to reinterpret the relationship connecting voice, singing, and body, for example, in Michel van der Aa's opera *One*. The composer, who is also a film and stage director as well as the writer and sound engineer of *One*, composes/stages/engineers the gap between the live and recorded voices of the singer.[3] The singer performs on stage as her image and voice is at the same time projected on screen, performing a different music, so that the (live) singer sings a duet, as it were, with her (screened) self (for elaboration see Novak, 2015).

The third mode, which I call *visual staging,* is often found in hypervisual styles of directing that pair the voice and the stage set. One example of this mode of staging is *Operation: Orfeo* (1993),[4] with music by Bo Holten, John Cage, and Gluck, libretto by Ib Michael, and set by Maja Ravn. Realized by the Danish ensemble Hotel Pro Forma and its artistic director Kirsten Dehlholm, *Operation: Orfeo* is abstract and is grounded in its stage and lighting design, a post-dramatic conceptual visual opera.[5] It is a 'reconceptualisation of the opera genre. Causal and dramaturgic sequence in libretto and music is replaced by a series of tableaux and compositions informed by purely visual and auditive principles rather than by dramatic modes of narration.'[6] The visual style accentuates the presence of voices, as for instance, when singing emerges from a picture frame as large as the stage itself, the inside of which is empty and pitch black. Singing seems to come from nowhere, from a black void—an aural illusion enhanced by the frame and the darkness.

Unsuk Chin's *Alice in Wonderland* from 2007, directed by Achim Freyer with costumes, masks and puppets by Nina Weitzner, is another example of *visual staging*. Rather than hiding, masking, downplaying or explaining the voices away, realistically or otherwise, the set matches the voices in kind. Puppets, disproportionally large masks, grotesque props and the peculiar set all function as elements equivalent to the voices. Heads are concealed under head masks which are huge in relation to the singers' bodies. Due to these head masks, facial expression is invariable and oddly separated from the act of singing. The staging is an example of the set enhancing the strangeness of opera's voices.

The fourth mode I call *choreography of the voice*.[7] It is typical of the styles of Robert Wilson, Pina Bausch, Sasha Waltz and others, in their association of opera's voices with gesture, movement and dance. Wilson combines a minimal and abstract set with slow, artificial, and highly stylized gestures. Together they bring out and emphasis static, artificial and estranged operatic singing. Wilson 'reinforces the elements that give a show its aesthetic, artistic and artificial character … [creating] beautiful and clear choreographic figures with honed and precise movements … [and] choreographic, heightened, theatricalized acting' (Pavis, 2013, pp. 289–90). Wilson conceives of his works in terms of 'audio landscapes' (quoted in Kolesch, 2013, p. 105), in which music forms its foundation.

Another example of *choreography of the voice* can be found in *5 Flutterbyes* by Anri Sala (2007), a work based on 'Vogliatemi bene, un bene piccolino' from Puccini's *Madama Butterfly*, Act I. The contemporary Albanian visual and inter-medial artist positions five lookalike sopranos (Butterfly) and two tenors (Pinkerton) to sing this scene from *Madama Butterfly*. We do not hear the voices singing together. Rather, the voice 'moves' among the singers, acquiring different voices/bodies en route. All the singers carry out the actions required to produce singing — breathing, moving their lips and enhancing their facial muscles—but they do not continuously let out sound. Only one Butterfly is heard at any given time (overlapping briefly with the voice of the singer handing over her voice), producing a live surround-sound effect.[8]

The pop-rock band OK Go can also be viewed as practitioners of *choreographing voice*. For example, in their video 'Needing/Getting', the band's four members, seated in a car, perform their song while the car hits, bangs, claps or otherwise plays on various objects it drives through. The sounds produced by the choreographed driving route form the music that accompanies their voices.

The fifth mode of staging the voice I dub *musicalizing matter*. Here I will use one of my own stagings, that of Erik Satie's *Socrate*, as an example. Folded paper is dropped into an aquarium filled with transparent liquid. Absorbing the liquid, the paper gradually sinks. The kind of paper, its weight, shape, number of folds, and the angle at which it is lowered into the liquid have all been meticulously designed. The paper's descent into the water is precisely calibrated with the rhythm of singing. The idea is to coordinate precisely the unfolding of the paper with the voice, so that the paper's movement would seem to be the *result* of singing and the music's pulse, as though voice has acquired power over matter.

The sixth mode of staging involves *voice as object*, *matter*, or *body*. Opera is sometimes conceived as a desire to achieve absolute autonomy for the voice, as a quest to attain the condition of voice-object detached from anything else. Opera can be seen as a means to fantasize an existence of voice alone. Despite its invisibility and ephemerality, voice would then acquire a peculiar material presence, as something in it or belonging to it would intimate mass and suggest a presence beyond itself. Voice would foster the notion that it has body and possesses a particular physicality, density or intensity. This body is conceived as a ghostly materiality arising and disappearing with the sound of the voice, or as that which leaves traces, remainders and echoes of an event. Victoria Hanna's performances on the whole, and 'The Aleph-bet' (2015) specifically, exemplify the mode of *staging voice as object matter or body*. In 'The Aleph-bet', Hanna explores the Hebrew alphabet as sound objects, shaping and carving the letters out of herself, it would seem. Utterance, vocal texture, diction are materialized, made corporeal, as with Connor's vocalic body, as if voices have indeed entered her body, affecting and reshaping it from the outside.

The seventh mode of staging voice is *in betweenness*. By this I mean staging the voice as an element in between different dualities such as music and text, music and the body, materiality and the abstract, estrangement and identification and so on. Voice would belong to both and neither of these terms and would be staged to involve the ambivalence. *In betweenness* is then an overarching notion that can involve all attributes of the performance. It has much in common with the notion of refraction of the voice, when features of the staging are informed by voice. The way I employ gesture in my directorial work may serve as an example. For I construct gesture as a kind of additional level of signification deriving from neither text nor directly from music while having affinities with the voice. The gesture is a bodily expression, a non-verbal means of communication stemming from the music but not illustrating it. Gestures may interrupt, slow down, and speed the effect of the music, they are acoustically driven elements that instruct the visual realm. Gestures are not attached to any character or action but rather establish a context and space, they pass between characters across scenes, lie between the vocal, the musical and the visual, they vary and morph.

The eighth mode of staging the voice I refer to as *vulnerable* or *exposed voice*. This mode of staging seeks to reveal difficulties in the production of the voice, as if it were heard in the workings, the strain, the fears of breaking down. Often in the operas I stage I transpose the vocal parts to a slightly uncomfortable range for the singer, or I ask singers to prolong notes and slow down phrases so that singing occurs on the edge, so to speak, when the air in the lungs is nearly drained. It is a mode of staging I have emphasized through the casting of the countertenor Doron Schleifer. Timbre, delivery, production, resonance, tessitura, grain of the voice, musicality—all are unique to this particular singer. In my staging I exhibit his voice by creating situations for it to sound alone, to emerge out of silence, to resound in the dark. Conspicuous among the features of Schleifer's voice is the vulnerability it projects. For me, the qualities of his voice are moving in and of themselves.

The ninth mode of staging I call *vocal disturbance.* Here I refer to all kinds of incongruences in the treatment of the voice that call attention to it: when a voice belonging to one performer is re-embodied in another, or when the voice of one is multiplied, divided or echoed in other performers. An example of what I mean can be found in Dominique Gonzalez-Foerster, *Opera, QM.15* (2016). The opera features a floating hologram in the dark of Gonzalez-Foerster as Callas. The artist constructs her hologram presence as a Callas lookalike. She is dressed and made up like the famed Greek singer. The voice however is Callas's. Gonzalez-Foerster lip-syncs to Callas's voice. The vocal disturbance is created not just by the conjoining of one (famous) voice with the movement of another body, but is also reinforced by the way the voice is sensed as emitted from a disembodied floating image.

The tenth mode of staging I dub *hollowed-out voice. Hollowed-out voice* occurs when what is staged are mere traces or remnants of the voice, often on the threshold of the audible. These traces may be whispers or breaths, voices drained of melody and timbre, as if they were aural shadows. An example of this mode of staging *hollowed-out voice* as combined with *composed staging* can be found in David Lang's *The Whisper Opera* (2013). Lang has composed such a quiet, entirely whispered work that the opera can only be experienced by a few listeners at a time. The listener must be very close to the singer in order to hear the nearly absent singing. This mode is closely related both to vocal disturbance as well as to the next mode of staging, which I call voicelessness. Whereas with the hollowed-out voice the experience is produced by acoustic privation, voicelessness is an experience of an alienation of the voice from the visual bodily presence.

The eleventh mode of staging I call *voicelessness* or *vocal muteness.* The sense of muteness is here produced by way of showing, viewing or pointing towards an instance of singing, while in some way being barred from participating in it. A recent example can be found in Marina Abramović's opera *7 Deaths of Maria Callas* (2020). While many of Callas' most famous arias are performed by other singers, it concludes with Maria Callas's voice being heard, for the first time in the opera. But this vocal event is visually alienating: Marina Abramović steps in front of the closed curtain as if she were, again, impersonating or embodying Callas. And indeed she mimics Callas's hand and facial gestures to the sound of 'Casta diva' sung by Callas. Abramović's mouth, however, remains closed: She holds back from lip-syncing in what I view as a staging of *muteness*.

2. Musicologist, director, choreographer

In *Staging Voice* I show how my ideas on staging have emerged out of a multifarious approach made up of theory and practice, manifesting the dual perspectives of musicologist and director. I stage my interpretations and, through my writing, interpret my own stagings. Having interpreted a work in order to direct it, I then reflect back on my own staging. My scholarship informs my staging, and my staging provides me with case studies that I can reflect on and interpret in my scholarly writing. As opposed to an all-encompassing hermeneutic approach, in *Staging Voice* theorizing receives its counterweight in the material concreteness of the process of staging the work, interpretations are articulated only insofar as they can be realized in performance, in voice and body.[9]

This dual perspective, enabled by the cohabitation of scholarship and directing, resonates with Patrice Pavis's notion of 'directing and its doubles' (2013, p. 283). The director necessarily takes on additional roles and functions, real and virtual, in the form of author, actor, choreographer, and so on. More often than not, a director assumes more than two functions. In my case, for example, the further role or disposition that I have adopted is that of 'voice choreographer'. That is to say: For me, the initial translation of the voice marks an entry into movement and a dispersal in space. Choreography transposes the voice's features into an array of movements of the body in space as well as into characteristic interactions with the stillness of the set. Indeed, my stagings are an outcome of working closely and from the very start with the designer on the set's conception. The varied chapters of *Staging Voice* will illuminate the deep ties linking the visual concept and the set design to the directorial work. The process of research, of devising movement, goes hand in hand with and is nested within the process of thinking space and the set.

The unique vantage of my book lies, as I have already suggested, in the ways my musicological research on opera informs and bears on my artistic practice as a director of contemporary opera. *Staging Voice* treats works staged by *TA OPERA ZUTA* (TOZ), an opera ensemble initially associated with Tel Aviv University. The aim was to work together—to place musicians, performance artists and designers alongside scholars from the arts and humanities—so as to research, interpret and perform contemporary opera. The first production mounted by *TOZ*, in 2010, was Kurt Weill and Bertolt Brecht's short school opera *Der Jasager* (The Yes Sayer). It was the culmination of a yearlong academic course in which the opera was studied in its musical, theatrical, cultural and historical contexts. Out of this process came an extensive booklet of essays and articles by students and scholars, as well as rare documents (encompassing, for example, a performance that took place in Palestine and Weill's short stay in Palestine). The disadvantages of working within an institution, however, were evident in the difficulty finding the necessary time to devote to the process, given the Music School's other projects and course load for students and professors. *TOZ* has continued its work since 2011 as an independent group.

3. Chapter outline

Staging Voice, therefore, is primarily a sustained reflection on three works that I myself have researched and staged: Bertolt Brecht and Kurt Weill's *Der Jasager* (1930), Valerie Whittington and Evelyn Ficarra's *The Empress's Feet* (1996), and Erik Satie's *Socrate* (1919), based on Plato's dialogues. Each work receives a lengthy, substantive chapter, with discussion that brings out a possible conception of what staging the voice might come to. The works considered are diverse in style, tone, and aesthetic. They share, however, a pronounced self-reflexivity and experimental character, and each aims to reconstitute a space for opera. Each illuminates a dimension of voice and points to what opera has become and what it has left behind. The three works share many common themes. They are each about death in that they form, as it were, an opinion about death. One work is devoted to the ethics of killing a child for the good of the community. Another work invites us to consider the benefits of dying as voiced in a philosophical doctrine. And yet another concerns itself with the symbolic death embedded within a long-held custom. In conceiving my stagings, these deaths were thought about in relation to operatic death. The three works also share an investigation of voice. They all experiment with refashioning voice, downplaying it, as is often the case in contemporary opera: One is a school opera that simplifies voice, one places all the stakes on a single, bare, unaccompanied voice, and one explores an under-expressive, confined voice. My discussion of the staging in each case includes references to documentations of the performances, which readers can watch on my webpage michalgroverfriedlander.com.

The first chapter is devoted to Bertolt Brecht and Kurt Weill's *Der Jasager* (1930). Brecht, one of the most important 20th-century innovators in theatre, created with Weill a work that attempts a radical transformation of opera. I analyse what the idea of *school opera (Schuloper,* related to Brecht's didactic plays) comes to and how it aims to recast opera's aesthetic, social and political function. The opera reflects on the notion of consent and on the victimization inherent in the demand for consent, and it does so on the basis of a tale that, via a child's horrific sacrifice, seems to continue opera's long tradition of having its heroines die. And yet Brecht and Weill precisely do *not* aim to immerse us in opera's tragic dimension; rather, *Der Jasager* seeks a kind of estrangement. I further trace the opera back to its origin in a Japanese tale and to Brecht's involvement with the Asian theatre of gesture. I consider how the different themes of *Der Jasager* can be taken as variations on a core of gestural content. Gestures also constitute the bridge to the staging and performance. In directing *Der Jasager* I have explored various possibilities of refraction and doubling of the voice through visible gesture and acrobatics, and through muting the voice and separating it from the body.

Chapter 2 is devoted to Ficarra and Whittington's *The Empress's Feet* (1995), a work for one unaccompanied voice. Conceived at the limit of what could be considered operatic, this work is challenging to stage. It possesses, through the voice, an almost hallucinatory force, and it invokes images, places, and movement that can be explored as emanations of the voice alone. Unfolding as a state hovering between wakefulness and sleep, *The Empress's Feet* recounts scenes of sleepwalking in which a strange bond is established between the voice and the wandering body. Its staging reflects this state of dissociation of voice and body, taking it to express something important about our experience of the voice in opera: The stage events and happenings are woven out of an invisible voice (a recording played offstage). The voice's power over the body is intensified by different performers, among them an acrobat whose hanging and walking in mid-air mirrors the hallucinatory force possessed by the voice.

In the third and last chapter, devoted to Erik Satie's *Socrate* (1919), I return once again to the relationship between death and voice. The opera, devoted to the ultimate teacher of philosophy, is based on extracts from Plato's dialogues (*Symposium, Phaedrus,* and *Phaedo*) and focuses on Socrates's final moments. I discuss in detail the work's conception and the context in which Satie composed it, arguing that he chose his particular excerpts from Plato's Socratic dialogues because hidden in each of them is a myth of the power of song: The excerpt from *Symposium* refers to the music contest of the satyr Marsyas and the god Apollo, the selection from *Phaedrus* to the myth of the cicadas' unceasing song, and the excerpt from *Phaedo* to the beauty of the swan's death song. In directing the work I bring to life Satie's imagination of Socrates as a philosopher-*musician* and problematize Socrates's expression of cheerfulness and equanimity facing death.

Notes

1 See also Gautier (2014), with an emphasis on her remarks:

> Listening appears as the nomadic sense par excellence and the voice as highly flexible, an instrument that can be manipulated to position the relation between the body and the world in multiple ways. [...] Listening is simultaneously a physiological, a sensorial, and an interpretative cultural practice.
>
> (pp. 9, 25)

2 For a recent example, see the staging of Samuel Beckett's radio text *All That Fall* (1957) by Pan Pan Theatre (running since 2011) and by Out of Joint (since 2016), both of which turn the radio play into a theatrical experience in the dark. See the discussion in Alston and Welton (2017, p. 4).
3 https://www.youtube.com/watch?v=bIsrOdrq8FQ 2:55–3:26 31.
4 https://vimeo.com/57213464 and https://www.hotelproforma.dk/project/operation-orfeo/ I thank Kirsten Dehlholm for her generous sharing of material about the project *Operation Orfeo*.
5 It is loosely based on the myth of Orpheus and Eurydice. See Campana (2019).
6 See https://www.hotelproforma.dk/project/operation-orfeo/.
7 The term *Vocal choreography* has been used but with different emphases. Initially, to my knowledge, the well-known choreographer and tap dancer Cholly Atkins coined the term *vocal choreography* in the 1950s, referring to a style in view as late as the 1980s. See Malone (1988) and Seibert (2019): Cholly Atkins choreographed sequences for pop vocal groups. The movements, the tap dancing of the group, were synchronized – the body doing something rhythmically different from the voices. His choreography was not meant to pantomime the storyline but rather to punctuate it. 'Atkins's choreography is characterized by precise visual polyrhythms' (Malone, 1988, p. 16). Atkins was known for accommodating the singers' need to catch their breath and to get back to the microphone on time and fit to sing. In addition, singing and dancing often require different uses of the body, especially breathing. Notice how Robert Wilson's choreography is slow, his gestures involving mainly the hands and arms, not legs or torso. The term vocal choreography, referred to as *voiced dancing, dancing voices*, and *dancing music*, has also been employed in connection to the choreographer William Forsythe (Vass-Rhee, 2010, pp. 409–10). The term has been used to account for 'aural-visceral rendering of corporeal significance' (Vass-Rhee, 2010, p. 391). *Vocal choreography* is also used when working with the sounds and voices emanating from dancers' movements. Microphones are

attached to the dancers' bodies, picking up sounds which then, in turn, are electronically manipulated and responded to by the dancers. *Internal choreography* is a term used by Nina Eidsheim (see 2009). Exploring vocal timbre and its relation to singing, the body, the listener, and race, she offers the notion of *performativity of vocal timbre*, viewing timbre not as inherent but as a mode of performance, as a set of *inner choreographies,*

> movements that create internal physical configurations that give rise to a timbral identity. Timbre, following this argument, is a physical configuration, and the resultant sound merely a confirmation that this internal shape has been performed. The relationship between vocal timbre, the body and race is a performed articulation connecting independent parts, rather than an expression of an essential relationship. But because the choreography that engenders timbre is internal, timbre has historically been considered the inherent sound of a body.

8 The work was presented at *'Il Tempo del Postino': A 'visual art opera',* co-curated by Hans Ulrich Obrist and Philippe Parreno, Manchester, 2007. https://waysofcurating.withgoogle.com/exhibition/il-tempo-del-postino-manchester. Sala explains the work:

> In 5 FLUTTERBYES this duet does not have only one Madama Butterfly, but five sopranos personifying her. When one soprano sings, the other sopranos mime the act of singing. The instant the singing soprano withholds her voice to continue only lipsynching, another soprano's voice takes over. They all have a different precise part when to sing or when to mute the voice, so that only one Butterfly is heard fluttering around in the space. I named it 5 FLUTTERBYES, because it is as if the sopranos become Madama Butterfly for that short moment when the voice flutters by. The Butterfly's presence floats in the room from one body/speaker to another, incarnated in the wandering voice. While remaining true to the narrative this proposal 5 FLUT-TERBYES seeks to investigate how the process of the choreographic movement of the voice through the space will at times serve or break the storytelling, creating a different encounter with the opera and its 'heroine'. During the performance the opera house was plunged into darkness, only lit by the fans of the Madama Butterflies, waving a light that flickered through the space and across their faces as they fanned themselves.
>
> (artist's Note in *5 FLUTTERBYES* presentation and score)

I would like to thank Noga Chelouche for introducing me to this work and to Jenny Verclas, the Studio Manager of Studio Anri Sala, for generously providing material about the work.

9 For a powerful analysis of hermeneutics in music scholarship, see Abbate (2004).

1 Staging a vulnerable voice

Weill and Brecht's *Der Jasager* (1930)

As I move into the chapters of the book devoted to the case studies of directing the voice, it might be worthwhile to remind readers at the outset that my work of directing is always informed by detailed research. Or more precisely, research and directorial work permeate each other reciprocally. And yet, for the sake of clarity, the chapters will be divided so that the first part lays out the results of my research and the underlying ideas behind the staging, whereas the second part of each chapter will discuss how this preparatory work forms the basis for the specific way chosen to direct the voice.

The underlying ideas, which is to say my concept for staging *Der Jasager* (The Yes Sayer), are informed by research into various contexts—musicological, philosophical, and literary—as well as processes of listening and dramaturgy and, not least, notions of opera and the singing voice. But if I were to stress initially an overarching theme, so as to give some orientation towards this chapter's complexity at the outset, I would stress how the task here is that of expressing the fatal ambiguity that is internal to the Yes-saying, or to the consent which gives this opera its title. One could equally speak of a duplicity that governs the conditions under which such consent is demanded.

This guiding theme will bring into play, in the staging of *Der Jasager*, several modes of *staging voice* out of the 11 I have outlined in the introduction. These modes will be particularly suited to express a voice that is overtaken by ambiguity and duplicity. I will be staging the mode of voice I called *in betweenness*. By this mode, I mean staging the voice so that it is neither in accord with the text nor quite with the music but rather exists as an element between music and text. Voice is also thereby pulled apart by the often tense relation of music and text. A voice that is caught between contradictory demands is a voice that is exposed in all its helplessness and vulnerability. So it follows that the second important mode associated with the staging of the voice in *Der Jasager* is what I call the

DOI: 10.4324/9781003187257-2

mode of *vulnerable* or *exposed voice*. This will be the voice of a child who is also a willing, assenting sacrificial victim. The direction of the voice is such that it leads to the climactic moment in which the child consents to his own sacrifice, a moment full of ambiguity, exposure, and fragility. The staging also introduces a third mode, what I call *voicelessness* or *vocal muteness*. The silencing or muteness of the voice is in fact its fate in this opera. At the peak of the opera, the exposure of the voice is intensified to the extreme. The staging, going beyond the direction of the score, lets the voice resonate as unaccompanied solo singing, wholly isolated and detached, prolonging it until the singer is out of breath and can no longer produce a sound. As though a voice were emerging from, and disappearing into, darkness and silence.

'Music… goes its own vast peaceful way'[1]

Der Jasager (The Yes Sayer) is an unusual opera, a one-of-a-kind experiment by its creators.[2] The half-hour composition is divided into 12 scenes, each self-contained and characterized by a different rhythmic *gestus*. Its simplicity is deceptive. Not what we would expect of opera, it is not an anti-opera either: It is situated well within the operatic world even as it is ambivalent towards such roots.

In the opera, the music adopts a unique stance towards what is happening on stage.[3] It neither sets the words nor tells of actions and emotions, nor is it solipsistic. Music does not establish characters: What the singers sing is not 'theirs' but is governed, indeed dictated, by the musical characteristics governing the *scene*, by an abstract configuration adhering to the rules of music. In *The Yes Sayer*, the text is not set to music. The music is neither ironic nor parodic, nor does it undermine the text (as is frequent enough in opera); rather, music engenders its own meaning. It is not simply that for both Weill and Brecht, music and text run independently of each other. Rather, each envisioned a distinct notion of music's role in the theatre.[4] For the composer, what is transcribed through music is something fundamental, unavailable in the text—something basic, like a tone of the human relationships presented on stage, stated musically.

Weill's statements about his collaboration with Brecht give us a glimpse of what he envisioned the role of music to be. In 1928 (two years prior to the composition of *Der Jasager*), reflecting on *Mahagonny*, the composer wrote:

> [T]he more powerful the writer, the more he is able to adapt himself to music, and so much the more is he stimulated to create

genuine poetry for music. [...] It [music] goes its own vast, peaceful way; it begins only at the static moments of the plot, and it can therefore preserve its absolute *concertante* character (if it hits upon the right subject matter). [...] music can reserve for itself its own independent, purely musical effect.

(Weill, 'Zeitoper', in Kowalke, 1977, pp. 483–4)[5]

For Weill, it is the writer who adapts himself to music. Music is independent and 'goes its own vast, peaceful way', following its own rules. Meaning is engendered in and by the music; music does not draw on meaning derived from the text, nor does it depict the text, it is distant from it. 'Absolute music was directly in a position to pave the way for genuine opera', writes Weill, 'for the musical elements of opera are no different from those of absolute music. In both it is only a question of the musical ideas unfolding in a form that corresponds with the emotional content'. Operatic music as absolute music engenders meaning as a result of its own rules (Weill, quoted in Kowalke, pp. 464–5). We find similar ideas in his article 'Busoni's *Faust* and the Renewal of Operatic Form' (1926), dedicated to his teacher Busoni. New opera should be formalistic, its meaning derived from form, just like a 'purely musical artwork' (quoted in Kowalke, 1977, 468).[6]

In *The Yes Sayer*, music does not support the surface signification of the text; it does not amplify words but rather derails them. Thus, I would claim, the music hands us the most profound meaning of the work.

Translations and transformations[7]

The opera is based on a 14th- or 15th-century Japanese Noh play,[8] which Brecht did not have direct access to when writing the libretto. He worked with a text twice removed from the Japanese source, and in the course of transmission the original work, *Taniko* (The Valley Rite) was substantially altered. Here is a synopsis of the Noh play:

> The master priest Sotsu no Ajari visits his youthful disciple named Matsuwaka to bid a farewell, as he is shortly to lead a group of *yamabushi* priests on a training journey into the depths of the mountains.[9] In *Taniko*, the master priest learns from his pupil Matsuwaka that the boy's mother is ill, and so he decides to drop in and see how she is doing. Learning of the master's imminent journey, the boy asks his mother for permission to accompany the master. The boy intends to pray for his mother's recovery

by undergoing the hardship of this journey. His devotion to his mother will be proved by such a journey, and divine help would be rendered in recognition of his devotion [...].

The boy's sincere appeal to the master moves his mother as well as the master, and the boy is allowed to accompany the group. On the journey, however, the boy develops a cold. Despite the master's attempt to hide this fact, the other priests eventually find out. In accordance with the law among *yamabushi* priests, anyone who falls ill at such a time will be hurled into a valley and buried alive.

Although he cannot stop his fellow priests from pushing the boy into the valley, the master refuses to leave the spot afterwards, claiming he is grief-stricken by the loss of the boy's life. His depression is so acute that he feels as if he were physically ill. He then asks the others to hurl him into the valley as well.

They understand his feelings and decide to pray for divine aid. The master priest joins the others, and they make an earnest attempt to solicit the aid of the great priest En no Mubasoku, the founder of this religious sect, and a great deity of Fudo Myo-o. They succeed in calling down a powerful deity, Gigaku Kijin. The deity carries the revived boy up in her arms and praises him for his filial devotion to his mother. After accomplishing her miraculous task, the deity flies away, hopping on the mountain ranges, and then disappears into the sky.[10]

In 1921, Arthur Waley published his translations of some 20 Noh plays from the Japanese. In his version of *Taniko*, Waley secularizes the play: Literal sickness is stripped of its symbolic meaning as spiritual impurity, the religious motivation for the boy's sacrifice is altered, and the journey's ritual purpose is decontextualized. Waley's substantial cuts include the deletion of four parts; roughly half of the original *Taniko* is left out. The most significant cut is the omission of the conclusion that followed the hurling of the boy down into the valley. Waley leaves out the priests' reluctance to carry out the execution in the Noh play and their strong emotional reaction to the situation. He also omits the suffering and unbearable sadness of the teacher which are caused by the boy's death; the priests praying for a miracle to bring the boy back; and the deity's restoration of the boy to life. All this is left out. In its place, Waley (1957 [1921], p. 235) inserts a footnote that contains an inaccurate summary.

The major change in Waley's translation is the cutting of the ending, as this omission totally alters the meaning of the play (Tatlow, 1977, pp. 180–9). In the context of the *yamabushi* sacred pilgrimage, killing the sick boy ensures that divine forces will not also punish the others with this sickness (Tsubaki, 1995, p. 164). Waley's cut distorts the play and renders it much crueller. Waley seeks to create an example in the service of an argument: *Taniko*, he explains in his short preface to the play, 'deal[s] with the ruthless exactions of religion' (Waley, 1957 [1921], p. 229). But in fact this follows only from his truncated version, in which the boy is dead at the end, the emotions of the characters are absent and the priest's request that his own death be brought down upon him has been deleted—not from what is contained in the whole of the original Japanese play.[11]

In 1929–30, Elisabeth Hauptmann translated Waley's English rendering of *Taniko* into German. Hauptmann's changes, though seemingly minor, are significant (Wirth, 1971, p. 610). Hauptmann downplays the religious elements of the Noh source even further and in the translation of the footnote notes only that the boy is resurrected (Tsubaki, 1995, pp. 161–78).

Bertolt Brecht then took up Kurt Weill's suggestion to write the text for a school opera (*Schuloper*) based on Hauptmann's translation. Brecht's text is very close to Hauptmann's.[12] Its sparse, simple, and exact language shows the indirect influence of the Noh's heightened prose (Wirth, 1971, p. 607).

In Brecht's play, everything turns pragmatic and goes through a process of socialization, secularization, and politicization. Pilgrims become students; the spiritual leader becomes the teacher; the temple disappears; the mountain ritual becomes the research mission or the quest for doctors, medicine or teachers (depending on whether the text is the first or revised version of *Der Jasager*); the boy goes on the journey not to pray for his mother but to bring her medicine; the mother is proletarian; the killing of the boy acquires a utilitarian rationale; and so on.[13]

Here is a synopsis of Brecht's text for the school opera: *Der Jasager* opens with the declamation of the Chorus that what must be learned above all is consent. The teacher arrives to bid farewell to one of his students before setting off to the city beyond the mountains, where he will seek a cure for a disease afflicting his town. At the student's house, he asks the boy why he has not been to school recently, and the boy replies that his mother has been ill. The teacher tells of his trip to the mother, who asks if he intends to take the boy with him. They agree that it is not a journey for children, but as he prepares to leave the boy asks to join the expedition. The teacher protests: The journey is too long and arduous. But the boy insists on going, so that he can bring back the cure to help his mother. His mother and the teacher reluctantly allow the boy to make the journey.

The teacher, the boy and three older students set out across the mountains. Soon the boy is exhausted and confesses that he is not well. The teacher tells him that it is forbidden to say such things on the expedition, but the three students, aware of the boy's condition, demand to speak to the teacher. When the teacher is forced to admit that the boy is ill, the students remind him of the Great Custom ordaining that whoever falls ill during the journey over the mountains must be hurled into the valley. The teacher acknowledges the importance of the old custom but reminds them that the sick person must consent to being treated this way. He asks the boy whether he consents to the custom or would choose instead to return to the village. The boy gives his consent, adding that he was aware of the risks involved when he agreed to embark on this journey. All he asks is that the three students fill his jar with the medicine they are to acquire and deliver it to his mother. The three students then throw the boy over the cliff, their eyes shut so that none of them can be deemed guiltier than the others. The opera ends with the chorus repeating its opening declamation: what must be learned above all is consent.[14]

The choice of text, as mentioned, was the composer's to begin with.[15] Indeed, two lines from Brecht's play that are absent from Weill's setting[16] shed light on Weill's conception of the notion of consent and raise the question whether Weill and Brecht shared a notion of consent and agreed on the meaning of the boy's killing.[17] The first deletion occurs in scene 4. In Weill's setting, the boy is not asked to agree in advance to everything that will happen to him on the journey. The second deletion is from scene 10, where, in Weill's setting, the teacher does not state that he would have been happy to die had he found himself in the boy's situation. This declaration is one of the focal points that underwent revision in each of the versions: In *Taniko*, the leader (in Brecht's rendering, leader and teacher converge) says that he would have preferred to die *instead* of the boy and not, as Brecht has him say, that he would have been happy to die *as* the boy does, that is, under the same circumstances. In Waley's translation, we find no mention of the wish found in *Taniko* to follow the boy to his death. Brecht has the teacher encourage the boy to consent by setting himself as an example of how to act. Brecht thus introduced a new dimension into the meaning of the boy's death, a dimension Weill leaves out. Through these deletions we obtain a glimpse of Weill's take on the notion of consent. The boy has not been prepared in advance for what might occur, and the teacher does not prompt him. Does Weill's notion of consent differ from Brecht's?

Consent

Although the composer establishes a clear, simple rhythmic profile in the chorus' profile that serves as the opera's *urgestus*, the text is ambiguous. While the rhythm is lucid, the impression of clarity and simplicity is misleading because the harmonic language is complex. Moreover, the blunt rhythm is not deployed in the service of the text; that is, it is not used to clearly set the words. As Ian Kemp points out, we cannot detect the key word 'consent' (1993, p. 147; see also Assaf, 2010). The scene is set as a choral canon in which 'consent' is obscured (see Music EX 1.1). Because different texts overlap, we do not hear what it is important above all to learn, nor what we should all agree upon. In the scene's last choral statement, in which the voices are in unison, 'consent' is covered up by a busy figure in the orchestra.

Music Example 1.1 The Yes Sayer by Weill and Brecht. Act I scene i, one measure after Rehearsal no. 2. European American Music Corporation and Universal Edition, 1930.

In Brecht's play, the chorus of consent, the assembly of bodies that speaks with one voice, is not repeated. The chorus is heard solely at the opening. In Weill's opera, the chorus of consent is heard at the outset, again at the opening of Act II, and yet again at the opera's end as its final scene. Weill repeats the scene as if it were a refrain or framing device that first states the terms of the narrative to be unfolded, re-instates them on the eve of the catastrophe, and reaffirms them after the fact. The chorus is repeated in the exact same way, textually and musically, on all three occasions. Kemp views it as external, labelling its three appearances prelude, interlude, and epilogue. He also inter-prets the chorus as a Baroque minuet, an opening gesture that is both distancing (since old) and welcoming (since familiar). This is in addi-tion to its tonalities of A and E that set it apart from the other scenes and the opera's tonality of D.[18] I would say that it can be heard as both external and internal. It occurs in structurally important places as a framing device (external) and refrain (internal). Harmonically it can be heard as external—not affecting the opera's establishment of the key of D, serving as a dominant and an upper neighbour to D—or it can be heard internally as a digression from the opera's main key area.

Weill's repetition of the opening chorus does not develop a musical feature. Absolutely nothing changes; this is repetition as such. Repeti-tion is not persuasion; the chorus' recurrence does not make it true or convincing—perhaps the contrary, it raises our suspicion. A statement that opens and then returns to 'lock' the piece is typical of musical rather than narrative forms and procedures. The composer, it would thus seem, reinstates the most important textual statement at the most important narrative junctures and sets the work's terms as musical: It is in music that we return to the initial statement, as we most often do, to convey unity, closure, fulfilled expectation. Thus, I would claim that Weill transforms Brecht's crucial statement into a musically signi-fying scene. Repetition shifts attention away from the text and towards the music, turning the statement on consent into a musical statement, into unspecified, non-discursive meaning. Music serves to empty the initial declamation of its intelligible meaning. Its repetition at the end, after the killing of the boy, is a trope of mechanical precision, stress-ing the act's emptiness and ritualistic nature. In these conditions, the agreement comes to nothing.

Brecht's most significant alteration to the Noh play concerns his em-phasis on *consent*. This is reflected in the use of the title *The Yes Sayer* rather than *The Valley Rite*. The Noh play tells us that the law stipu-lates that anyone who falls ill, and thus is no longer able to continue the spiritual journey as a pure participant, will be hurled into the valley.

Brecht adds the twist that makes all the difference: The social custom demands that he who is to be killed must consent to the sacrifice. Brecht adds an opening chorus deliberating the notion of consent:

> What we must learn above all is consent
> Many say yes, and yet there is no consent
> Many are not asked, and many
> Consent to wrong things. Therefore:
> What we must learn above all is consent.[19]

This opening choral account, however emphatically stated, is ambiguous. It emphasizes the importance of learning to consent 'above all'—but what does one consent to? Even when saying 'yes', there is no consent—why? The conclusion of the passage is circular and does not follow from what precedes it; rather, it reiterates the opening line.

In the course of the play a form of consent is deliberated that is both voluntary and coercive. A boy is to be asked whether he consents to the Great Custom that demands his death. A teacher declares that the law requires that the boy be asked what should be done; yet the boy *must* comply, must respond with 'yes' and agree to his murder. Asking the boy to consent, then, is meaningless:

> We will ask (they asked) him whether he wants us (wanted them) / To turn back on his account. / But even if he should want us (wanted them) to do so / We will (they would) not turn back / But throw him into the valley.[20]

The boy consents, and the students repeat after him that which has been derived from their inducing the teacher to effect the boy's answer. Everyone and everything is directed at prompting the boy to acquiesce.[21]

Due to the reception of and responses to the opera, as well as the questions raised about the meaning of the moment of consent, Brecht decided that *Der Jasager* needed a counterpart.[22] Weill, his relationship with Brecht by then on shaky ground, refused to compose music for the second part. Brecht slightly changed *Der Jasager* (in particular altering the context and rationale for embarking on the journey) and added a companion piece *Der Neinsager* (The No Sayer), thus forming a pair of didactic plays that were to be staged together.[23] *The No Sayer* is, up to a certain point, almost identical with *The Yes Sayer*. Yet, crucially, the boy does not consent and as a result is not killed. The reversal of the death sentence is achieved by the boy's somewhat sophistic reasoning about the conditions that allow one to change one's mind about a prior agreement and withhold consent.[24] Brecht presents us with a notion of consent to oppose, and my claim is that Weill's music does precisely that. When Brecht sought Weill to compose music for his revised *Yes Sayer* and for *The No Sayer*, Weill refused. Perhaps for Weill the music had already stated its position: The opera is simultaneously the yes and the no. This I take to be the meaning of consent once the music is introduced.

Yes and no

Der Jasager is a school opera that is part of the corpus of Brecht's didactic plays. The genre has elicited much scholarly discussion as to its nature, scope, and didactic means and aims.[25] These considerations are further related to debates about Brecht's Marxism and his socio-political agenda and their entwinement with his aesthetic inspirations and artistic innovations. *Der Jasager* introduced innovations in theatre, music, and opera, such as the casting of schoolchildren and the performance targeting the performers themselves. These innovations were coupled with Brecht's aim to produce estrangement as well as his use of techniques that thwart the audience's (and the actors') identification with the characters on stage. It is within this broad political and theatrical context that one must assess the meaning of consent in the opera.

How is one to weigh the options of saying yes or saying no? Is the opera teaching that one must withhold consent from the societal demand of sacrifice for the greater good? Is *The Yes Sayer* the terrible vision to which *The No Sayer* constitutes an answer (though not in music)? This is a common way of reading the relation between opera and play (or between the two plays). Yet one ought to consider more carefully the constitution of the contrast between affirmation and negation. Several preliminary and very general considerations should clarify the difficulty involved.

First, given Brecht's Marxist convictions, it is possible that he construes the two plays to be a form of dialectical antithesis. The possibility of extracting oneself from a social deadlock presented in each play requires a dialectical negation – that is, one does not find the 'right' side; rather, one takes a broader view that regards both resolutions as partial. The didactic aspiration lies in the audience's working towards the position from which to negate the very absoluteness of the opposition proposed in both plays. Viewed from a higher ground, what seemed like an exhaustive choice really isn't. That is, the problem of choosing between consent and dissent can disappear by addressing the conditions that lead to the demand to make a choice in the first place, one need not take a side.

A second point concerns the notion of consent. Consent forms the centre of the understanding of political community, primarily in what is known as social contract theories. A society's form is justified by being represented as a possible outcome of a unanimous agreement from an imagined condition called the state of nature. Thus, questions about the fundamental order and nature of a just society would be considered through thought experiments devising what the state of nature is and what kind of order would be achieved by a unanimous agreement out of that state. Social contract theories form the core of liberal political philosophy. But they have notoriously been criticized by Marx and Marxist political theorists. Stressing the element of consent reduces the problem of society's formation to a matter of choice by individuals who are characterized as having certain essential properties of humanity, namely the properties attributed to these individuals as imagined in the state of nature. In particular, such theories attempt to justify the social order by reference to the isolated individual, who must reach a decision about the benefit of the social bond as such. Such an idea of consent and choice does not account for the essential social and historically situated condition of human existence. It masks the conflict at the basis of social forms of existence between opposed social classes, whose development is historical and dialectical.

The third preliminary consideration concerns the translation of affirmation and negation into the theatrical sphere. More specifically, if one asks where in theatre a sacrificial logic would be in play, one would think of tragic theatre. Fate, in tragedy, is the state of being caught in a field constituted by ambivalence, by implicit opposed demands. If one is not aware of the opposed demands, if they are not written laws but are, so to speak, implicit in one's mode of existence, then an impasse will be repeated again and again. Repetition, often associated with being pursued by fate, is precisely the state where there is no single univocal law, and your actions feel precisely as though every step taken in one direction throws you against the opposite demand, in a process that recurs endlessly back and forth.

The understanding of fate implies that such repetition is implicit in the form of life unless a new and definite law arises for all. But the possibility that such a new law would emerge depends on the visibility of the conflict of the opposition implicit in the sphere of life. How is this opposition made visible? Tragedy is the understanding that the tragic hero, through his embroilment in the field of fate, makes visible the internal contradictions of society. The impasse made visible through his sacrifice makes society aware of its contradictions. The individual, so to speak, makes manifest in his body these societal contradictions, concentrates them within his life story, or arrests the back-and-forth movement of innocent life that gets entangled in fate. The ability to make visible the contradiction is the precondition of its dialectical overcoming in a new order or a new regime of law. Thus transgression, sacrifice, and atonement are central to this scheme of the formation of the law.

Of course, a fundamental element of Brecht's theatre, and therefore of Weill and Brecht's opera, is opposition to the tragic logic in theatre and opera. Brecht proposes an epic theatre that sets itself against such tragic logic. The epic tells a story from a distance, as it were, which allows the audience to feel as though they are observing a world from the outside. It is not identification that is the fundamental effect of theatre, but rather what Brecht calls estrangement [*Verfremdung*]. Estrangement, surely, is not emotional disconnection. Yet even if events on stage are sad, terrible, or grotesque, they must not involve identification. They must appear as parts of a world closed in on itself that provokes astonishment at the ways and conditions under which those belonging to it function. Only the relaxed investigation of these conditions can lead one back to the understanding that they are ours.

The Yes Sayer presents consent as both voluntary and coerced. A boy is to be asked whether he consents to the Great Custom that demands his death. A teacher declares that the law requires that the boy be asked what should be done; yet the boy *must* comply, must agree to his death by saying 'yes'. Asking the boy to consent is part of the ritual, yet his fate is never in doubt. The boy consents. Everyone and everything is directed to prompt the boy to acquiesce. The conditions for the answer were established long before the boy was asked to choose.

How does Weill set this moment in music? How is both the solitary choice of the individual and the coercion that is driving the inevitable response experienced? Weill has composed nothing extraordinary, and the music here is not in the slightest way different from what is heard prior to or following the boy's 'yes'. The music is only reduced to single instruments, as though forming an intimate exchange between the teacher and the boy: One instrument, a repeated two-bar figure, an ambiguous, unresolved harmonic motion. Identical orchestral music is heard for the solicitation and the inevitable response that follows, for the question and reply; the same music is employed to quote the law and to signal compliance with it, to prompt and to be prompted.

The orchestral music, in other words, signals the 'intimate' moment of choice or decision but does so in a way that makes clear its complete *continuity* with the irrevocable unfolding of fate in all that preceded it. It can be said to reveal something of the truth of this moment, beyond what the characters (including the boy) take it to be.

The boy's 'yes', the drama's goal and very purpose, is a solitary exposed note. The opera's unrelenting stress on rhythm is halted. The note is not repeated, reverberated, refracted, or multiplied—as is every other moment in the opera. The moment is rendered unique, the 'yes' delicate and frail. The accompaniment is present before and after the boy's single note—leaving the bare 'yes' to emerge starkly out of the silence. The singer's difficulty in executing this note reflects its importance.

Yes-singing and mute agreement

The opera presents a challenge to performers which stems from, among other things, the limits it imposes on expression, the independent meaning derived from the music and the uncertainty as to the classification of the singing style and types of voices it calls for.[26] One of the fundamental directorial choices made in this production was to remould the singing voices.[27] The unease induced by Brecht's play was exaggerated in this staging by the use of refined and precise singing, which was beautiful on the one hand but distanced, reportorial and therefore disturbing on the other. The singing was built not on lyricism but primarily on repetitive rhythm. The emphasis on voice staging led to the decision to work with opera singers rather than with actors, the latter often cast in Weill's works. The operatic voice—artificial, unnatural, stylized—seemed apt for depicting characters who were not fully developed. In particular, the artificiality of the countertenor voice trained in early music produced a disembodied, sourceless, asexual effect. The voice's ability to express the unique world of *The Yes Sayer* was explored via acoustic effects such as humming, buzzing, droning, singing 'too close' to the audience (placing singers in the audience) and singing from different places in the theatre, as though the voice were indeed sourceless, a mere echo, or had been dubbed.[28]

We treated the voice as if it were an instrument, as if it were not communicating a text or as if it lacked understanding of the words it sung. We aimed at a solipsistic voice, a detached object independent of character, the singing body and the meaning of the text. We created a problematically expressionless singing that was unaware that it served as a messenger bearing a horrific tale. Moreover, some of the singers were cast as mute doubles, making it hard for the audience to distinguish the mute from the audible performers. For example, in the trio we dropped the accompaniment, and the voices sang a cappella. We cast five singers, yet only three sing – the child, the mother, and the teacher. The doubles of the teacher and the child engage in lip-syncing. The effect is a kind of aural illusion. It confuses the dependence of what is heard on what is seen, even as it conditions the mute performers' relation to the set and the masks. In their surroundings, the mutes are not consistently perceived as being voiceless. They are a presence lying somewhere between singing bodies, orchestral voices, stick masks, and the inanimate set. The indistinguishability of those who have a voice and those who are mute comes to connote the problem of implied consent in social life—the way consent exists by opposition not being voiced or, worse yet, when the potentially dissenting voice arrives too late, because agreement has tacitly been settled beforehand.

Doubling and muteness

The introduction of mute doubling is part of the broader theme of doubling that is at play in the opera's characters and set. Doubling confuses the identification of voice with a specific character or an emotion, as in traditional opera. Doubling here took the form of adding an actor and splitting a part between two voices. The cast included two children rather than a single child (the part divided between or doubled by them). There were four students instead of three, and the teacher was doubled by an actor. Different voice colours were used, in particular by casting two countertenors (mother and teacher), thereby erecting a further rift separating what was seen and said from what was heard. Another such disturbance occurs because sopranos sing the boy's part. Thus, the meanings emerging in this staging resulted significantly from decisions concerning the *staging of voice*.

One character was not doubled but acted, so to speak, as her own double: the mother. In the libretto, she appears only in the first act but in our production she was left on stage in the second act, as a mute presence, almost as part of the set. It should be noted that in the original Noh play the same actor plays the mother and the spirit who revives the boy at the end. Added in Weill and Brecht's version is an element of duplicity in the mother's role. Though she goes through the motions of attempting to stop her son from joining the expedition, she also plays her part in agreeing to what feels like a preordained ritual with a known outcome.

Another mode of doubling occurs with the stick masks taking the form of an abacus. The monstrosity of an 'education' that leads to students and a teacher throwing the boy off a cliff is concentrated in the abacus masks of the chorus. Each member of the chorus has a different variation of the beaded face. The masks can also be seen as stick figures that are extensions or silent doubles of the chorus. The chorus' make-up divides their facial features into geometrical abstract shapes, defacing them, while the calculating masks become placeholders for the human presence (see Image 1.1).

Muteness at some time or other affects all of the opera's doubled characters: The second teacher, the second child, the mute presence of the mother in the second half, and the acrobat throughout (discussed below). The child-double, for instance, is a prophetic version of the child, acting out future consequences in the present. What is sung is acted out mutely. The doubles, shadows of the singers, rarely break into singing. But when they sing, they do so in crucial moments, for example, when the child-double blocks the mouth of the child with a shadow-play gesture, stealing the voice and singing in its place (see Image 1.2). The mute bursts out in song in an attempt to alert to the danger of what is about to be played out in song. The doubles also

Image 1.1 The Yes Sayer. Performers doubled by stick masks in the form of an abacus. Photographer: Michal Shanny (Performers: Yeela Avital, Anat Czarny and David Feldman).

Image 1.2 The Yes Sayer. Stealing the voice. Photographer: Michal Shanny
(Performers: Yeela Avital and Anat Czarny).

stand for the story's repetitious ritualistic structure: This tale has re-
curred and will recur over and over again. Their inherent muteness
points to a core muteness in the voice.

Death

Finally, consider the doubling that is essential to the moment of death.
In the original *Taniko*, the overturning of death is the deity's divine act,
and the boy's miraculous reward at the end seems to be the purpose
of the journey, indeed of the play. The power of this death is revealed
in its potential to be reversed. In Waley's translation, the meaning of
death is reassigned when the spiritual aspect is downplayed and the
boy is not resurrected. Death is rendered incomprehensible, its cruelty
overemphasized by the further omission of all emotion. Death is the
culmination of the play. Brecht, by drawing attention away from the
murder and towards the notion of consent, recasts the significance of

the boy's death. The assent to the boy's killing is here a social event that serves as a didactic lesson about the community's role in relation to the individual. Should the individual learn to adhere to the community and its rules, learn to sacrifice himself for the benefit of society? For Brecht, the meaning of this death is not religious purity; it is the realization of society's ruthlessness.

At the end of the opera, a chorus sings a justification for the killing. The sounds of the boy's death are quickly replaced by sounds conveying the moral principle that led to it in the first place. The chorus is familiar, and its music is catchy. This death has left no mark on the opera; it is pushed aside by the music of social reasoning: The boy's consent is the rule; he himself is insignificant. The chorus sets the terms for how to conceive the unfolding events, and at the end it returns to signal that nothing, in fact, has really transpired. If, after the boy is killed, the initial statement about consent is repeated, then this killing has made no difference and has had no effect other than as an example of an abiding social principle. This makes the opera more ominous than any of the earlier versions of the play.

Weill's reiterated chorus complicates rather than clarifies the killing. What does consent stand for at the end of the tale, after the boy's killing has been witnessed? What does the return of the chorus do to our response to death? Does not the death's renewed justification render even this performance and our critical response powerless?

In our performance, the sociopolitical statement is implanted in the aesthetic—in the unnatural beautiful operatic voice. One realizes that the killing has been performed by and in these voices. Instead of individualizing and isolating the moment of death, the staging refracts it via various transformations in the different figures: First multiplied in the deaths of the child doubled by two singers, it is further re-enacted through the introduction of an acrobat. Upside-down, the acrobat gradually descends from high above to the ground. She lies on the floor and joins the dead children. Finally, the death is shown as an unfolding, schematized shadow-play via a stick-figure representation of the child, viewed as a show within the opera. This multiplication of the moment (not counting the multiplication of the scene by the mirrored floor) is a means of draining death – not of its horror, but rather of its tragic sense of individuating authenticity. Death is replicated and reproduced in the social conditions that dictate the narrative and is in no way a tragic sacrifice that is the child's own fate.

The staging only hints at what occurs without filling in the libretto's gaps: A story was not constructed, a narrative was not created, characters were not given depth or motivations for specific actions. Everything was to remain abstract and to echo in an incomplete, schematic, unparticular way: There was to be no history, sense of origin or psychology, and so what was approximated were the conditions of music itself.

This conception in the staging could be realized by the creation of movements, motions or gestures comprising an in-between stratum that could convey the work's textual, musical, visual, and vocal dimensions. 'In' neither the text nor the music, the gestures functioned as part of an additional signifying system that brings to the surface the strangeness of the text, the music and their interaction. Gestures stem from the music but interrupt and affix it by freezing, slowing down and speeding it up (gestures are slower than the tempi of the music in the static, claustrophobic first act, and faster than the tempi in the second, steady-walking-on-the-journey act). The gesture is an acoustically driven element that instructs the visual realm, resulting in an image that intercepts what is heard. It hints at the ways we are unaware of the acoustic instruction of the textual, dramatic, and visual.

The opera, as mentioned, is divided into 12 self-contained scenes, each characterized by its own rhythmic *gestus*. The depiction of the characters is subordinated to that of the scene. When the scenes change, so does the rhythmic world and the depiction of characters. Atypically in the operatic world, the characterization of the opera's dramatis personae is subject to the characterization of the scenes; moreover, this characterization is mainly rhythmic. In other words, the characters themselves are not distinguished from one another but rather change according to the scene's soundscape. The space surrounding them is defined musically, so we get a background in which the characters act. Essentially, *The Yes Sayer* has no characters in the operatic sense, since no one is given particular vocal or musical characterizations. Instead, the scenes, each only several minutes long, take shape around a musical and gestural axis.

The *gestus* is a complex and multifaceted term defined differently by Brecht and by Weill.[29] In his essay on Brecht's Epic Theatre, Walter Benjamin characterizes gesture via the understanding that 'the more frequently we interrupt someone engaged in acting, the more gestures result' (Benjamin, 2003, p. 305). The internal relation established between the concepts of gesture and action provides a productive starting point, distinct from other ways of analysing the gesture in terms of bodily expression, as a bodily language or a non-verbal means of communication. If we begin with the action and form of the gesture from its arrest, we would tend to read the gesture's meaning in and via the aim of the action that was arrested. But we can also start from the gesture's endpoint and consider how meaning opens up from this concluding locus. This reversal of direction does not necessarily lead back to the action, whose arrest can have the power of opening up a dimension of meaning unavailable in the consideration of the action itself. Attention to the gesture can serve to indirectly illuminate *the surroundings of meaning* that might be veiled by the unity of the utterance itself. This way of thinking of gesture—as illuminating or giving a certain tone to its surroundings—relates to Weill's often neglected understanding of the gesture in music. For Weill, *gestus* is the social 'rendered' musically; music in the theatre neither illustrates the text nor advances the action but is expected 'to capture and to realize the gestic character of a succession of situations'. For Weill, through music and especially through rhythm, something fundamental to human relationships transpires.

Three kinds of gestures pervaded TOZ's production: crossing hands, bending, and slouched walking. These gestures served as an additional system present alongside those of the opera's text and music. Inspired by Weill's use of the term *gestus* as a musical and particularly as a rhythmic essence, they are not attached to any character or action but rather establish the work's context and space. Gestures pass between characters across scenes, lie between the musical and the visual. Unlike the opera's characters, they have depth and vitality; they vary and morph – in them, meanings are established.

Each of the gestures engulfs within itself a doubling around a certain axis of symmetry. The first is the gesture of crossing the palms of the hands. Initially, it serves to project a shadow of a flying bird. It is child's play: The gesture is formed by each hand holding on to the other hand's thumb, whereby the fingers become wings in a bird's arrested flight. The shadow-play gesture signals self-absorption, a solitary game in sparse surroundings, as when a child is alone in the dark. The gesture requires no object, only darkness and light. An archaic form of theatre, little hands throwing a shadow. The shadow projected by the gesture forms an initial echo with the set design's limited black-and-white colour scheme—as though bidding us to enter a two-sided, two-dimensional, doubled world of light and shade.

The gesture that starts as a sign of childhood and childness transforms itself from being a shadow-play of the continuous flight of a bird to become the disjointed, contorted wringing of hands in tortured doubt (of the doubles of the teacher and the child), leading to the use of the crossed palms to silence doubt, to the crossing of masks by the big chorus reproducing the crossing of the hands as a gesture of overlapping consensus, and finally to the crossing of the hands on the body as a gesture of death. The opera's opening gesture, the innocent children's shadow-play, foreshadows the horrible end. The shadow-play indeed turns into a large unfolding slideshow depicting the child being cast down into the valley (see Images 1.3–1.4).

The second gesture is a backward or forward bending of the body's upper part so as to form an angular break of the upright position and the body's vertical axis in space. The gesture problematizes uprightness as determining the axis of bodily symmetry. It opens up the question of a body's proportions: Where is the body's midpoint? Where is its centre of gravity? Where are its weak and susceptible joints? Such questions are also raised by the body of the acrobat suspended in mid-air. This gesture refers to the unspecified sickness that ignites the tale, a sickness afflicting all. For nearly the entire first act the mother holds this posture, embodying the gesture. She is positioned leaning back. She is 'inside' her lodgings and is 'higher' than it, she is inside and behind it. The gesture's near-permanent presence in her posture disrupts the vertical lines dominating the set. The second gesture of bending the upper part of the body also occupies a space of transformation

Image 1.3 The Yes Sayer. Shadow-play gesture. Photographer: Michal Shanny (Performers: Yeela Avital and Anat Czarny).

Image 1.4 The Yes Sayer. Shadow-play gesture. Photographer: Michal
Shanny (Performers: Kfir Levy, Jonathan Opinya, Efrat Raz and
Hemi Levinson).

and meaning: The bent posture of the ailing mother is exposed as part
of her body and not, as it might have seemed at first, a gesture she
makes. Furthermore, this bending is transformed by the teacher into a
farewell greeting (as when one bows in departing) in one of the few moments of compassion in the opera. In the chorus's movements, bending
becomes the threat of the inhuman or the automatic in human encounter. The first and second gestures merge when the students call out to
the child, establishing the fact of his illness and the implementation of
the custom.

The third gesture is associated with walking: A rhythmical slump-
ing from left to right divides the body's movements in two—the left
shoulder raised, the right shoulder lowered. The division of right and
left forms another axis of bodily symmetry. This gesture brings together the journey with the way that it does not lead to a new place
but rather unfolds the consequences of what has already been agreed
upon. It translates, so to speak, the pace of advance to a raising of the
left and then the right shoulder while the body walks in place.

Voice and gesture release the work from direct text-music dialec-
tics. The staging creates voices and singing that are independent, as

it were, of the music and the text, inventing gestures as an element in between music and text that belong to neither. This staging of the opera is meant to contest acquiescence and to echo with the original Noh play and its ultimate overturning of the boy's death.

Acrobat, measure, distance, scale

There is a fundamental relation between the gesture and the theme of doubling and repetition. Indeed, one might say that a gesture creates a doubling within the space of a character's presence. It provides a space to detach one's observation from the living present and investigate, as it were, what is happening on stage from outside. The gesture is part of Brecht's epic third-person theatre. Repeatable gestures problematize identification and provide the estrangement, the distance that is essential to the detached investigation. One might also characterize gestures as schematized actions, articulate and repeatable units that can construct and transform meaning.

Schematization and abstraction, even flattening, raise at the same time the threat of illusion and the difficulty of finding a proper measure or scale to regard what is happening in the social realm. Can perspective and distance be achieved in relation to society? Can sufficient concentration and abstraction from the flow of life give us the proper schema to assess its conditions? The notions of the schematic and of proper scale were of fundamental importance to our stage design. Typicality and schematization are first related to the theme of shadows that is central to the design of the opera. For a shadow provides one with only the recognizable contours of things. The original gesture that opens the opera serves to cast a shadow-play and is echoed in the design of the scene at the end in which the boy is thrown off the mountain to his death—which is represented as a shadow-play.

The issue of schematization and scale is further presented via the characteristics of the surroundings, whether the house or the mountain. The house's rooms are schematically represented by a pair of Necker cubes, which produce the illusion of depth and three-dimensional space from a schematic two-dimensional drawing. The Necker cube, importantly, produces a certain kind of optical illusion. You can see it so that it faces either upwards or downwards.

Schematics, scale and the translation from two to three dimensions are also at work in the representation of the mountain as a schematic, three-dimensional topographic map. Doubling and miniaturization are evident when the drama on the mountain is sung by one of the children; the other sits next to the mute mother and plays at climbing on the mountain in miniature using a 'doll' scaling the three-dimensional topography. This is related further to the choice of the design and direction of the opera to locate the house and the mountain at the same place—hinting that the proceedings already contain something of the preordained sacrifice, that the killing on the mountain slope had already been decided on at home.

Schematization is also a matter of the depiction of the characters. It is important to note that the opera's characters are types rather than well-defined individuals. There is the teacher, the boy, the mother, and the students. The types lack depth or inner complexity. Very little is known about their backgrounds, and most of what we know concerns the general condition, a sickness, that affects them all. The costumes further schematize the characters, erasing the differences in the body's contours, effacing gender, distinguishing characters solely on the basis of role ('teacher', 'student', and so on), adding an abundance of black to the already monochromatic colour scale of the stage. The thick, non-flexible rubber from which the costumes are made inhibits movement. Each movement creates its distinct fold in the rubber, as though motion can temporarily mark itself on the costume, as though the costume itself were gesturing. What is promoted is a sense of scale or a gradation of sameness spanning the opera's characters from the child to the chorus. They are variants of one another.

Schematization can open up the possibility of distance, allowing a type of abstract and detached overview. This possibility is epitomized in the role of the acrobat, who reproduces the enigmatic lexicon of the gestures in concentrated fashion (without the 'story', so to speak). The acrobat's position is of an abstraction that sees only gestures. The acrobat acts as the opera's listener, witness and reflection, and is its über-double. She embodies nothing but gestures in the sense that all her movements are construed out of the language of these three gestures; as though astonished to witness them from above, she attempts to decipher their meaning by repetition, by adopting the behaviour they proscribe and by altering them according to the requirements of her hanging body (see Image 1.5). In her, the opera is schematized into a succession of gestures. These gestures are neither interpreted by the acrobat nor are they a commentary on what we see and hear. They come across as embodiments of her perplexity and bewilderment, emphasized by her muteness. The performers' voices and gestures are translated into the voiceless gestures of the mute acrobat. The role of the acrobat is to provide an overview of the performance, a condensed compendium of the gestures we are presented with. The distance of the acrobat raises the question of what it means to achieve the proper

Image 1.5 The Yes Sayer. Acrobat mirroring gesture. Photographer: Michal
Shanny (Performers: Reenat Caidar Avraham, Jonathan Opinya,
Hemi Levinson and Efrat Raz).

perspective on what is happening in the opera. It raises the question of
what it would be to have something like the proper measure or scale in
relation to the intricacies of social life.

The staging of the opera undermines acquiescence. The child's consent, the frail 'yes', is staged as the singer's difficulty in executing and
producing the note with which to voice this agreement. The moment
is staged as if it were an expression of voicelessness. The mode of staging, of *voicelessness* or *vocal muteness*, is employed to bring out the act
of singing even as this very singing signifies muteness and to an even
greater extent, being silenced.

Notes

1 Kurt Weill, 'Zeitoper', trans. Kim Kowalke, in Kowalke, 1977, pp. 483–4.
   Originally published in *Melos*, VII (March 1928), pp. 106–8.
2 For intriguing discussions on Weill's opera see Albright, 2000, pp. 170–4,
   177–80; Assaf, 2010; Calico, 2008, pp. 16–42; Drew, 1965, pp. 934–7, 1987,

pp. 226–9; Humphreys, 1988; Kemp, 1993; and Sheppard, 2001, pp. 83–95, 249–50.

3 For an interpretation of *The Yes Sayer* and its music as 'prompter', see Grover-Friedlander, 2011b; for a variation of the interpretation presented in this chapter, see Friedlander & Grover-Friedlander, 2012.

4 For a discussion of this topic, see Borwick, 1982. For Brecht's ideas about music in theatre, see, for instance, his 'On the Use of Music in an Epic Theatre', and 'On gestic music', in Willett, 1966, pp. 84–90, 104–6. On Weill's different notion of *gestus*, see Weill, 'Topical dialogue about *Schuloper*', in Kowalke, 1977, pp. 520–6.

5 Weill's essay was originally published in *Melos*, 7 (March 1928), pp. 106–8 (all citations from Weill in this chapter have been translated by Kowalke). On Brecht and Weill's collaboration, see Harden, 1972.

6 Weill's essay was originally published as 'Busonis *Faust* und die Erneuerung der Opernform', *Jahrbuch Oper* (Vienna: Jahrbuch 1926 der Universal-Edition, pp. 53–6). The notion of opera as a purely musical form appears in several of Weill's writings. See also his 'Concerning the Gestic Character of Music', in Kowalke, 1977, pp. 491–6, originally published as 'Über den gestischen Charakter der Musik', *Die Musik*, 21 (March 1929), pp. 419–23.

7 For elaboration on the text's various iterations (prior to its transformation into an opera) and for an alternative interpretation of the opera, see Grover-Friedlander, 2014, pp. 381–404.

8 The author is anonymous, according to Keene (1970, p. 316). Arthur Waley attributes the play to Zeami (14th century) in his 'Preface' to *The Nō Plays of Japan* (Waley, 1957 [1921], p. 5). According to Wirth (1971), the play was written by Zenchiku in the 15th century.

9 The *yambushi* are ascetics who combine Buddhism with Shinto practices and mountain worship. They are believed to hold magical powers. *Yamabushi* priests, or mountain ascetics, are religious believers who commit themselves to a physically taxing way of life in the mountains for days at a time in order to absorb the essences of nature and so become powerful. Some *yamabushi* return to the secular world and engage in acts of healing, using their nature-energized power for the benefit of others. See Keene, 1970, pp. 316–7.

10 The synopsis is found in Tsubaki, 1995, pp. 163–4. See also Tauber, 2010.

11 Waley also leaves out the names of the two main characters that in the original carry meaning. The boy's name, Matsuwaka, is tied to his fate and is constructed from two parts: '"Matsu" means pine tree, and "waka" a young boy, an ending attached to a name of a young male child. A pine tree symbolizes everlasting strength and long life' (Tsubaki, 1995, p. 165).

12 We can only assume that Brecht came across the brief summary of the ending, but decided, following Hauptmann and Waley, to leave the ending out; indeed, he did not have a translation of the original's ending to work with. It is unclear how aware Brecht was of the alterations made to the Japanese play, and whether this mattered to him.

13 For details on Brecht's changes, see Tatlow, 1977, esp. pp. 180–9, and Tsubaki, 1995.

14 *Der Jasager* was to have its premiere during the music festival 'Neue Musik Berlin 1930' but was withdrawn (by Brecht and Weill) because of the festival's rejection of Brecht and Eisler's *Die Massnahme*.

15 For textual changes made by Weill, see Kemp, 1993, pp. 143–57.

16 That is, they are absent from the text accompanying the score. Weill made the changes after Brecht's text had been separately published; thus they appear only in the score and not in Brecht's text. These lines are also absent from Brecht's revised version of *The Yes Sayer*, which means that Weill's setting might have influenced Brecht's revised play.

17 On Weill's notion of consent, see Drew, 1965, and Humphreys, 1988.

18 On the harmonic language of the opera, see Assaf, 2010, Humphreys, 1988, and Kemp, 1993.

19 Brecht, 1985, p. 63. I used this translation—though it is a translation of Brecht's revised version of *The Yes Sayer* since the chorus in the two versions is identical. To my knowledge, there is no English translation of Brecht's first version.

20 Brecht, 1985, pp. 6–68. Though this is a translation of Brecht's revised version of *The Yes Sayer*—I used it since for this part of the play the two versions are identical up to the last line I quote. In the revised version, Brecht's last line reads: 'But let him lie here and go on'. The translation of the last line in the first version above is mine.

21 For an interpretation of *The Yes Sayer* as related to the notion of prompting and the operatic prompter, see my 'Prompting Voice in Opera' (Grover-Friedlander, 2011b).

22 *The Yes Sayer* was hailed by fascists and condemned by the Left. This response, claims Wirth (1971), is why Brecht rewrote it and added as its complement *The No Sayer*. Wirth argues that a comparison should be made not between *The Yes Sayer* and *The No Sayer* but between the revised *Yes Sayer* and *No Sayer* taken together and the first version of *The Yes Sayer*. For greater detail, see Wirth, 1971, pp. 613–5.

23 Weill composed only two interpolations for the revised version of *The Yes Sayer* (after the earlier version of *The Yes Sayer* was published). See Kemp, 1993, pp. 149, 155–6.

24 For a comprehensive comparison of Brecht's three versions, see Tauber, 2010.

25 On the didactic in Brecht see, for example, Jameson, 1998. On the *Lehrstück*, see, for example, Kalb, 1995. For school opera, see, for example, Drew, 1965, Hinton, 1994, and Rockwell, 1986.

26 On singing Brecht, see Kowalke, 1993.

27 Directed by Michal Grover-Friedlander in cooperation with the stage design of Eli Friedlander, the production in question was originally performed as a culmination of a year-long course at Tel Aviv University in 2010 devoted to *Der Jasager*. The following year, the opera group TA OPERA ZUTA was formed. The group is committed to integrate research and performance of opera and music theatre, concentrating on the specific questions raised by the staging of the voice. TA OPERA ZUTA's 2011 performance of the opera can be seen on my webpage michalgroverfriedlander.com/performances/theyessayer-weill-brecht-2011.

Director: Michal Grover-Friedlander. **Stage Design:** Eli Friedlander. **Masks:** Eli Friedlander, Ofri Omer. **Lighting Design:** Iris Mualem. **Costumes:** Meital Gueta, Moran Sanderovich. **Make Up:** Miri Shamash. **Translation and Text Setting:** Yaniv Baruh. **Conductor:** Bar Avni. **Performers:** Teacher: Doron Schleifer. Child: Yeela Avital. Mother: David Feldman. Doubles:

Anat Czarny, Jonahan Opinya. Acrobat: Reenat Caidar Avraham. Students: Efrat Raz, Kfir Levy, Hemi Levinson, Jonathan Opinya. Chorus: Tal Bergman, Maayan Goldenfeld, Shahar Lavi, Hanna Bardos, Noa Hegesh, Haggai Grady, Yoav Weiss, Pavel Pivnev. Piano: Yevgeny Yontov. Flute: Avner Geiger. Clarinet: Hila Zamir. Saxophone: Orr Guy. Violin: Tamar Koren, Daniel Ratush. Cello: Ben Shibolet, Daniel Mitnitsky. Double Bass: Or Shemesh. Guitar: Nimrod Gilboa. Percussion: Almog Turner. **Correpetition:** Yaniv Baruh. **Production:** Michal Grover-Friedlander, Yaniv Baruh, Noa Hegesh.

28 The different experiments led us to place the orchestra in the centre of the stage, close to the voices, without our knowing that this had been Brecht's placement. His reasons might have been motivated not directly by the acoustics but rather by the wish to expose the mechanics behind the scene.

29 For Weill on the *gestus*, see above, fn 6. On *gestus* in Brecht and/or Weill, see Calico, 2008, Fiebach, 2005, Friedlander, 2005, Jameson, 1998, Morley, 1986, and Pavis, 1982.

2 Binding the voice

Ficarra and Whittington's *The Empress's Feet* (1995)

As in the first chapter, I begin here as well with reflections on the given opera's context and background, the research which has oriented my interpretation and, which, in turn, inspires and impacts staging.[1] The second part of the chapter will be devoted to staging and the different modes of the voice involved here. Since the context encompasses discussions of foot-binding and somnambulism and the tradition of the castrato in opera, it will be apt to introduce an overarching theme to orient the reading. How is one to stage the voice in an opera that is a dream state? What *is* the voice in an opera that is entirely dream throughout, from beginning to end? A dream is closed upon itself. There is, for the dreamer, no exterior to the dream. Moreover, the dreamer is not quite a specific character in the dream but rather finds herself all through the dream, reflected, as it were, by things and by figures. The voice makes manifest this condition. The opera *The Empress's Feet* is entrapped within voice. The *Empress's Feet* truly holds us inside its dream world and its voice, which is nowhere and everywhere. One might feel confined to the work's small dimensions and its repetitive and unreal world; entrapped within one voice; caught within a process that is circular, unending and set wholly apart from reality.

In dream, things are deformed, fragmented and also strangely lacking in substance. The opera provides the opportunity for the mode of staging voice that I call staging the *hollowed-out voice*. There are moments in the opera *The Empress's Feet* in which the voice dissolves into whispers, residues and faint echoes drained of timbre. These sounds or sound-traces are on the threshold of the audible and comprehensible, as if they were oral shadows. The whispers, to take an example of one type of hollowed-out voice, are magnified on stage via dim near-dark lighting. In these surroundings, the strain of hearing whispers experienced by the audience corresponds to the difficulty felt by the performers in producing and projecting them.

DOI: 10.4324/9781003187257-3

A voice for the feet

The Empress's Feet (1995), with music by the composer Evelyn Ficarra and a libretto by the writer Valerie Whittington, is based on a children's tale from 1946 that traces the tradition of foot-binding to an origin in a pair of large, disobedient feet. The Chinese tale on which the opera is based is centred on a sleepwalking Empress with enormous, beautiful feet.[2] The tale revolves around the Empress's restricted awareness, her reduced consciousness and inability to recall what exactly her feet do. The feet take over in sleep, when consciousness is dimmed. Consciousness migrates to the lowest part of the body; the feet, transformed into independent beings, are given a will of their own, after which the rest of the body, puppet-like, follows. An independent will is attributed to them: 'My feet,' said the Queen, 'want to walk' ('The Empress's Feet', 1946/1961, p. 43). It is they who are responsible for carrying the body away at night. In the tale, these sleepwalking feet are blamed and then 'punished' by being operated on and 'trimmed': To release the sleep-walker from what have become regular nightmarish walks, the feet are submitted to a procedure that reduces their size. This intervention, miraculously, is painless. Not stumps but new, tiny, beautiful feet are formed. An operation rather than a lengthy process of deformation solves the problem of wandering, opinionated feet. In the fairy tale, the transformation of the Empress's large feet puts an end to her sleepwalking. But, newly graced with small feet, the Empress becomes envious of women whose feet are now larger than hers. An ensuing proclamation from the Emperor prohibits any woman from having feet that are larger than his wife's. Years of ongoing foot mutilation become a miraculously quick and painless instant. The gradual processes involved in binding—bodily distortion, mutation of shape, inhibition of growth—are contracted into a single brief, painless event. The custom's onset is made an expression of the envy felt long ago by one woman. The gorgeous large feet of this one woman become exquisite tiny ones for all. The diminutive foot, now made into a symbol of prettiness, is enforced on all women.[3] The children's tale, an origin myth for the thousand-year Chinese tradition of female foot-binding, accounts for the adulation of small feet by providing these extremities with a glorious mythic past.

I argue that *The Empress's Feet* is an opera that provides a voice for feet and for their movements; an opera that makes feet sing. Here feet are transformed: They move not by walking but by sleepwalking. The opera's expression of the theme of sleepwalking is evident in the strange bond it forms between body and voice, or more specifically between a body wholly controlled by its feet and a singing voice. In the opera feet possess a will of their own, a nocturnal power over the body which gives them a voice. *The Empress's Feet* imagines singing as an expression of sleepwalking feet which voice their will to walk. The emanation of the voice is estranged, belonging not to the mouth but to that particular body part that generates movement, that extracts the body into motion: The body's lowest part, the terminal point of the legs, which forms the basis of our postures and positions, of standing, walking, moving (Madhaven and Nair, 2013, p. 151).

The Empress's Feet

The opera *The Empress's Feet* is radical in its employment of the voice in translating its source tale into song. It is composed for a single bare voice. More broadly, it is cast for a single unaccompanied singer possessing an exceptionally wide range. Furthermore, the opera adds a figure called *A Singer*. In a state hovering somewhere in a zone encompassing sleepwalking, storytelling, singing, dreaming, and wakefulness, *A Singer* is at once dreamer, sleepwalker and minstrel. *A Singer* tells us of an Empress's marvellous feet and sings their praises; *A Singer* dreams, forgets, awakens, remembers, sleepwalks, runs, has nightmares, as if the voice is the Empress's even as it is *not* hers. It is as if what surrounds the Empress, as well as what resides within her mind—places, situations, actions, states of mind, other characters— reside within that one voice. *A Singer*, an all-encompassing voice, embodies everyone and everything.

In the preface to *The Empress's Feet,* co-written by composer and librettist, Ficarra and Whittington describe their opera:

> A woman dreams and dreams about a woman who dreams... A sleep and a forgetting. A sleep and a remembering. A dreamer wakes and tries to reconstruct from the fragments in her memory the story she has read and has found recurring in her dreams. In time and space far removed from her waking world.
>
> (Ficarra, 1995)

The opera nests dreams inside dreams, so that one is uncertain whether anything occurs outside sleepwalking: We are immersed in 'a state that is not quite reality, a state in which identities are less permanent and more permeable, where the object of the "plot" [...] is to explore, to be confused, to hover in a strangely timeless world...' (Ritchey, 2010, p. 183). The opera is a dream that 'comes in parts [...]

each night'. A dreamer, a woman, *A Singer* is remembering a dream about an Empress with enormous feet; in turn, a dream resurfaces in *A Singer*'s memory through song; *A Singer*, dreaming of an Empress, receives an Emperor's call to sing the praises of an Empress's beautiful outsized feet, but then an Empress's nightmares are also those of *A Singer*. *A Singer*, as dreamer, is at once within and beyond a dream world. It is the singer who dreams a sleepwalking Empress, is a witness to the operation performed upon her inside her dream, is an Empress undergoing a cutting and is a singer praising an Empress's feet. Whom are we listening to? Who in the opera hears *A Singer*'s song? Is a listener construed along the lines of *A Singer*? Who sings, sleepwalks, dreams and retains the residue of dreams?

The changes made to the tale—so that all nests within the condition of sleepwalking and all exists as singing—are connected. Sleepwalking in the opera is not a scene within the story but rather is the frame of *The Empress's Feet*, permeating everything in it. The opera does not retell the fairy tale through singing but transforms storytelling itself through song, precisely to address the difficulty of telling a tale in a state of sleepwalking. A story is remembered and forgotten, hovering between states of consciousness and not anchored in any subjectivity; it shifts temporalities as it is enacted, as it recurs; it is reconstructed and recounted. A story is fragmented by the condition of sleepwalking, out of which *A Singer*, invented by the opera, sings of the attempts to draw out the story and her position within it. Telling, enacting, dreaming, singing are embodied in voice.

I claim, then, that in *The Empress's Feet*'s circumscribed self-enclosed space of dream-and-nightmare, nothing exists that is not derived from the voice. It is memory and illusion, speaking and walking, the materiality of breath and unaccountable pain. Feet acquire a life of their own and become the counterpart of the singing voice, what it conjures as its own image. The opera traps us inside its voice and provides no escape route. We are caged within the confines of the work's tininess, narrowness and internal repetition; we are entrapped within a voice. Caught within a process that is circular, unending, and estranged from reality.

The Empress's Feet does not employ the operatic voice as such. Its voice is not larger-than-life, eccentric, extreme, extravagant, exaggerated, excessive, grotesque, bizarre, irrational, or absurd. The opera does not construct a voice that lies at the limit of human capacities or borders on the unnatural. There is neither a display of superhuman pyrotechnic virtuosity nor a parade of special production techniques, that takes pride in the feats it achieves without technological intervention. It is not an exercise in concentrated intensity, imparting throughout an impression of ease, flawless technique and over-the-top, emotionally charged execution. But neither does *The Empress's Feet* partake in the aesthetics of the opposite camp, as it were. It is not a straightforwardly avant-garde piece; it is not experimental, post-operatic or anti-operatic in an exhibitionistic way. In fact, it confines itself markedly within its own musical language. It remains seques-tered within restricted, self-imposed borders. The scenes form variants of one another; text, music and units of music-and-text are reordered, fragmented, varied, reiterated and ornamented. Changes are minute and predominantly limited to small ornamental figures along a toned-down range. Though the opera fosters a multiplicity of vocal personae within its single voice, it does so modestly, for example by employing hidden polyphony (that is, a narrow range is kept intact within each vocal line, while a wide range is reserved only for keeping the opera's vocal personae apart from one another). *The Empress's Feet* is humble in its use of vocal effects: The slight bending and muddying of the voice, and mostly breath-induced effects that suffocate or enhance the production of sound.

The opera is constructed with modular units of music-and-text that are reiterated, curtailed, cut, pasted, fragmented, repositioned or oth-erwise displaced and relocated; it is built on scenes that are repeti-tions and variations of one another (see Music EX. 2.1). Character, action, and dream are indistinguishable. The compositional technique enables music to override text; that is, units of music-and-text behave musically and call for a musical sort of listening. Sound, timbre, pace, rhythm, tempo outweigh sense.

There are 12 short scenes, each between one and six minutes long, that together amount to roughly thirty minutes. The opera simulates

Music Example 2.1 The Empress's Feet by Ficarra and Whittington. Scene i
'A Woman Wakes', mm. 1–5; Scene xi 'She Wakes', mm.
1–5. London: Contemporary Music Voices, c/o British
Music Information Centre, 1995.

a truncated work, one halted in the midst of a breath. The impression of incompleteness mirrors the opera's plot, itself a juxtaposition of fragmented memories and bits of dreams, walks, and songs. The compositional technique is aligned with the work's subject matter in its offer of unanchored experience to its audience. Text and music are shared throughout; time, space, consciousness, identities, dreams are conflated. This fosters an ambiguous and unreal quality in the opera, where everything is porous, hovering, timeless.

Repetition of that which belongs to a sphere removed from our consciously guided actions and understanding is, indeed, what serves to make sleepwalking permeate the entire space of the opera. Sleepwalking exhibits an understanding through repetition rather than through conscious awareness of, and active engagement with, one's surroundings. It is not the daydreaming that makes conscious existence more fluid and pliable but rather something that, through repetition, brings out something other in human gestures and embodied existence. Put slightly differently, one could say that there are things the body can do only by being dissociated from the control of consciousness and by being allowed to realize itself in a space figured otherwise. This can be further clarified by briefly considering the accounts given sleepwalking in the 19th century.

Sleepwalking feet

The restriction of sensory impressions in sleepwalking, and the effects such restriction would produce, have fascinated scientists throughout the ages. The somnambulist would experience only those sensations that pertained to the specific action being performed. During an episode, the sleepwalker can walk, talk, eat, and act violently, endangering herself and others around her—punching, grabbing a knife, and shooting off a pistol (Stiles, Finger and Bulevich, 2010, pp. 794–6).

The eyes, though usually open, do not see. Memory also seems to function in a particular way. The sleepwalker appears to have separate memory tracks that remain unaware of one another: While awake, the sleepwalker remembers nothing of what had occurred during a sleeping episode but remembers such events during an episode, as though possessing a dual memory: One branch of memory working during sleep, the other while awake (Stiles, Finger and Bulevich, 2010, p. 795).

Up through the Renaissance, sleepwalking was viewed as a species of possession, divine or diabolic, as well as a unique ability and the opening to secret knowledge. In the 18th and 19th centuries, French and German scientists experimented with artificially inducing an altered state of consciousness known as 'animal magnetism', exploring what they came to term 'magnetic somnambulism'. Schelling understood this condition to be a state in which central wakeful consciousness retreats to reveal the separate intelligence of particular organ parts.[4] Somnambulists, regarded as clairvoyant and possessing the ability to discover hidden knowledge inaccessible via other means, were employed in the service of advancing scientific knowledge. Viewed as being free from temporal and spatial restrictions, they were taken to have access to the past, present and future. In a somnambulistic trance, matter, space and time were transcended. Unbound from the body, the soul—termed 'flying soul' and possessing the power to travel faster than electricity and even voyage to other planets—could transport itself anywhere. Its special abilities were understood to be based on forces of electricity and magnetism. The somnambulist, usually a woman, became an instrument in a scientific investigation conducted by the magnetizer. The therapeutic situation was divided between the powers of the somnambulist and those of the magnetizer who induced magnetic sleep (Feurzeig, 1997, esp. pp. 229–30). Magnetic somnambulism was at once employed for healing (through the ability to see inside a body), for gathering information through extrasensory perception, telepathy and precognition, and for theological explorations of extraterrestrial realms. The latter aim was devoted to the pursuit of gnostic knowledge or magnetic gnosis 'with claims of direct access to a superior knowledge pertinent to dimensions of reality beyond the domain bounded by material reality, space and time' (Hanegraaff, 2010, p. 120). A somnambulist was believed to possess some kind of internal sense through which she could access the underlying nature of reality and existence. Mesmerists conceived of a duality between daytime consciousness and night-time consciousness: The former is limited, whereas the latter is wider, deeper, and

> grounded in an expanded consciousness to which we gain access in dreams and other altered states of consciousness, such as the somnambulic trance, and in which we find ourselves liberated from the narrow limitations of time, space, and linear causality.
>
> (Hanegraaff, 2010, p. 128)

Along these lines it was believed that true and superior knowledge was to be found in sleep. Highly gifted somnambulists were 'sleep specialists' or 'sleep virtuosos', expert in 'using altered states of consciousness with a superior degree of sophistication, so as to take advantage of their full epistemological potential' (Hanegraaff, 2010, p. 133). Such notions led to late 19th-century theories of cerebral automatism or unconscious cerebration, referring to a physical process involving the activation of the cerebrum during dreams and waking hours. In this view, somnambulism is believed to result from a strong current of unconscious cerebration, which 'prompts the sleeper to rise from his or her bed and perform actions usually done while awake' (Stiles, Finger and Bulevich, 2010, p. 803). In the late 19th century,

> the sleepwalker symbolized a central controversy of Romantic medicine. If behaviors involving higher brain functions (such as speaking, writing, or sensory perception) could be accomplished automatically by sleeping persons [...] then the regulatory power of the soul or will appears questionable.
>
> (Stiles, Finger and Bulevich, 2010, p. 804)

These ideas led ultimately to Freud's conception of the unconscious. Sleepwalking figures in important ways in the development of models of the unconscious mind. Hypnosis as practiced during the initial stages of psychoanalysis is analogous to artificially induced sleepwalking, with mesmerism being a scientific-theatrical version of this process.

This fin de siècle period was a time of vampire tales such as *Dracula* (1897), whose eponymous protagonist induces somnambulistic trances in his victims, and hypnotist fables such as George du Maurier's novel *Trilby* (1894), whose Svengali fully controls the artist's model Trilby, whom he transforms into a singer:

> Falling under the spell of a malevolent despot, these young heroines relinquish volitional control and with it the ability to check, account for, or even recall their actions. ... [They] become other than themselves, other to themselves, abrogating self-control as they obliviously transgress, like automatons, moral, social, racial, class, and sexual boundaries.
>
> (Cucullu, 2009, p. 305)

Lois Cucullu shows how these seduction episodes depend on somnambulism and take place during an episode of altered consciousness. It is a state portrayed by the novels as impressionable and susceptible, leading to violent and fatal consequences for the women: 'these somnambulist fictions mobilize sleep, that most private and subjective state, and turn it from a restful condition into its opposite in order to represent what they deem women's latent desires' (Cucullu, 2009, p. 306).

The underlying fascination with sleepwalking for Romantic and Victorian writers entailed frightening theological implications: 'sleepwalking ominously suggested the possibility that the human body and brain could function mechanically, without the guiding power of the soul or will' (Stiles, Finger and Bulevich, 2010, p. 790).

A nocturnal phenomenon, somnambulism is linked to the time reserved for opera's heroines, all those who are drawn to the moonlight, know they are about to die, and sing their deaths. Singers and sleepwalkers possess a mysterious affinity and share various characteristics. The latter's automatic speech and mechanical gestures echo the 19th-century notions of the virtuosic singer: An automaton, a soulless machine dedicated to technical display.

Against this background, one may inquire into the character of sleepwalking scenes in opera. The association of sleepwalking with the spectral, or with the haunting of the world, recalls the operatic or vocal presence of sleepwalkers in works such as Verdi's *Macbeth*. Whereas *Macbeth* conceives of sleepwalking in terms of the remnants of the past obsessively performed instead of the waking consciousness of the present, another opera, Bellini's *La Somnambula*, suggests the identification of sleepwalking with a certainty that stands over and above any wakeful presence of mind. Amina can stride confidently, a virtuoso walking on a narrow path over an abyss, where anyone conscious of the situation would be quick to fall. In different ways, both Amina and Lady Macbeth transgress modes of representations of desire. Amina sleeps in the bed of a man who is not her husband; Lady Macbeth imagines herself smashing the skulls of her unborn babies. The famous sleepwalking scenes in these operas (lesser-known examples occur in Bloch's and Sciarrino's *Macbeth*s (1904–6; 1951)) are reenactment scenes. We are witnessing one of several occurrences. The scenes themselves centre on repetitive motor gestures and a process of constant motion for which the voice, as it were, is the outcome. Indeed, sleepwalking scenes are marked by an unusual rendition of singing. Verdi's scene, for instance, is innovative, refusing to adopt the vocal conventions of either mad scenes or death scenes and thus undermining both. The composer calls for an ugly and hollow voice, for a singer predominantly engaged in acting. Lady Macbeth's gestures erase invisible stains; she alone sees a derailed pantomime. Verdi composes obsessively repetitive orchestral gestures that sound more vocal than the singing voice, unsettling the sound of singing. Albright uses the term 'anti-aria' (Albright, 2007, p. 182). Amina's extraordinary vocalism, the coloratura display, is uncharacteristic of Bellini's reform opera of the time.[5]

Sleepwalking Empress

Given this account of the suffering and the power associated with sleepwalking, we can now return and re-describe the transformation that the opera *The Empress's Feet* brings to the fairy tale's portrayal of sleepwalking. In the fairy tale, sleepwalking is associated with nightmares and is viewed as endangering the Empress. In the opera, sleepwalking also allows the Empress to wander and dream of freedom.

In the fairy tale the Empress has been walking at night since she was a child. When the Emperor learns of these sleepwalking excursions, he follows her: 'The Emperor feared that Ti Chin might fall or hurt herself, so he caught up with her, put one arm around her waist, and with the other covered her mouth lest she should scream upon her awakening. And sure enough, Ti Chin was frightened and struggled, until she awoke and saw it was her husband who held her' ('The Empress's Feet', pp. 41–2). The Emperor's first suggestion is to tie her ankle to the bed with a golden chain. That night, the Empress has a nightmare in which she is wandering, looking for her husband. She fails to find him. A dragon then attacks her—attacks of the sort that the Emperor had earlier tried to protect her from. In the fairy tale, the Emperor comes up with a new suggestion for the cure of his wife: Reducing the size of her feet and cutting nine inches off of them.

The onset of the Empress's nightmares are an outcome of the enforced restrictions on her feet, which have been tied and so barred from walking at night. When she is prevented from sleepwalking she becomes afflicted with bad dreams about these excursions. Indeed, the fairy tale offers a negative portrait of the phenomenon of sleepwalking, linking it to night terrors and violence. The opera, on the other hand, introduces a scene in which, as a reaction to the operation on the feet that puts an end to sleepwalking, *A Singer* loses her voice. Once the feet no longer will the body to walk somnambulantly at night, and so no longer enliven and animate it, the voice does not sing; once the feet have been operated on, the voice fails. One realizes that in the opera the voice is not solely telling tales: Its character as singing voice is intimately linked to the contingency of the feet:

> I try to sing. /But my voice gets weaker. /I try to run. /But my feet won't move. /The Empress's feet. /I see her /I try to sing. /The Hall is /I see her feet /I try to /Five Miles...

The loss of voice ruptures the narration. It is a momentary collusion between the voice reduced to songlessness and the operated-on feet.

It suggests that the autonomous wilful feet are bound to the voice. In the opera, although the operation on the feet initially results in a loss of voice, it leads ultimately to the opening of a space of fantasy, to the singing of the fantasized homecoming of the Empress.

In the opera sleepwalking also serves as placeholder for dreams of freedom. The opera radicalizes the predicament of the independent feet by constructing a new ending. Rather than following the tale to its end, the opera sides with the feet. It concludes with a dream that restores the large feet and the splendour of their walking. Imagining feet that are strong, broad and long, their huge strides once again audible in the dark. The fantasy that human embodied existence is pliable cannot be fulfilled without inflicting violence. But the opera's last scene is also a radiant moment of wish fulfilment, when, as if in a dream, the Empress returns from far away, carried home by her enormous, beautiful feet.

Foot-binding

Making sleepwalking central to an origin story of foot-binding yields a tale that hides the horrors of a body part's gradual deformation. It also empowers the feet with activity, special abilities, a gift of self-walking. The fairy tale constructs a set of specificities regarding when and how walks occur, and in this it parallels how foot-binding conspicuously causes movement to be laboured and painful, thus producing a certain gait. Among the traditional explanations for foot-binding as a practice is the view that small, lotus-shaped feet were erotically charged (with emphasis placed on the fetishizing of delicate slippers and shoes) or were meant to imitate the feet of dancers performing on a lotus flower; alternately, foot-binding has been seen as a route for upward class mobility or as evidence of a strong-willed character as shown through the endurance of pain; finally, it has been regarded as a way to restrict women from straying too far or from participating in hard labour.[6] Explanations for the custom can be divided into four categories. The first is the symbolic, in which foot-binding is viewed as emblematic of the castration of women. Freud held this view, as is mentioned in Julia Kristeva's book *About Chinese Women*:

> Freud saw in the custom of foot-binding the symbol of the castration of women which Chinese civilization was unique in admitting. If by 'castration' we understand the necessity for something to be excluded so that a socio-symbolic order may be built—the cutting off of one part of the whole, so that the whole as such may

be constituted as an alliance of homogenous parts—it is interesting to note that for Chinese feudal civilization this 'superfluous' quantity was found in women.

(Kristeva, [1974]/1986/1991, p. 83)[7]

The second rubric for explanation is the aesthetic, which emphasizes that the practice turns mutilation into beauty. The third is the economic, which views the tradition as a means of masking the value of female labour. Lastly, a socially oriented explanation focuses on class mobility and the possibility of marrying up. In fact, Dorothy Ko (2005) argues that foot-binding was not only a painful immoral practice but also a form of mother-daughter bonding: Entailing lifelong daily maintenance, foot-binding provided a mother with the role of ensuring the continuation of what has been seen, perhaps misguidedly according to Ko, as a means of victimization.

In fact, the search for origins, the vagueness of what can be found and the invention of origin discourse have all helped establish the meanings of foot-binding as such. Scholars place the practice's origin as far back as the 3rd century B.C. or alternately the 3rd century A.D., or even as late as the 10th century. Eighth-century tales and ballads describing spying on women dancing with their socks cast off offer images of seduction and sensuousness. If these accounts attest to the origin of foot-binding, then it was not initially associated with chastity but rather regarded as morally dubious and would in fact have been condemned. But it is unclear whether the practice emerged before the 10th century. From the 15th century onwards, we find multiple accounts that place the source of the custom in the 10th century. Evidence to support these descriptions is for the most part unknown or unverifiable.

Indeed, there are numerous kinds of foot-binding, which have over time acquired multiple and contested meanings:

> Footbinding began as an act of embodied lyricism—to live as the poets imagined—and ended as a ridiculous exercise of excess and folly. In the final analysis, self-contradiction—the ability to encompass conflicting desires and the tendency to turn against itself—is the only enduring trait of footbinding as a social practice and as a subject of knowledge. For this reason, it continues to both repel and fascinate long after it has ceased to be a viable practice.
>
> (Ko, 2005, p. 229)

The bound foot became the focus of meticulous acts of definition and measurement, and footwear intended to enhance its allure was duly fashioned. Depending on the historical period, the primary emphasis was placed either on an ideal arched shape or on size. Measurements and artificial corporality were fetishized. In addition, binding produced a fixation on exteriority and décor—shoes and slippers, textiles, embroidery and ornaments. There were various fashions in shoes, slippers and leggings, as well as embroidery and adornment. Indeed, because the bound foot is known only by its exterior shape, size and outward packaging, it provides no clue as to the flesh underneath. What conceals the foot is fetishized and perceived in isolation from the female body. Ko identifies changes from what we find in the 16th century, when female footwear was charged with erotic connotations, to evidence from the 17th century—predominantly through allusions in poetry and drama—that the foot itself became the erotic object. She shows how foot-binding can incite the imagination: A body part that is hidden serves to generate sensual fantasies. Unseen, the bound foot becomes an object of male enquiry, allure and desire. The 17th-century writer Li Yu, in his essay 'Hands and Feet', provides a description of the bound foot: 'The feet of Lanzhou women measure at most three inches, some even smaller. Their steps are agile and quick—like flying—sometimes outpacing even the men' (quoted in Ko, 2005, p. 152). In the 18th and 19th centuries, foot-binding was essential to Chinese definitions of womanhood. At this time, a further change can be detected: Though a strong taboo against exposed feet remained in place, no longer was there a preoccupation with a passive decorated entity detached from the body. The foot was returned, as it were, to the realm of the body. The feet's attraction became tied to gesture and posture and to its movements. Binding alters the posture, shifts the foot's centre of gravity and produces a mincing gait that was praised, prized and eroticized as 'lotus steps'. The way a woman walks, as an expression of both gait and anatomy, became central: Her step ought to be small, slow, dainty, deliberate, agile. The stylized foot is lauded as an improvement upon nature—reshaped, remoulded, gauged, masked and made to move otherwise.

The violence inflicted on the feet, producing the small lotus shape, is a perverse aesthetic wonder. Strangely enough, it has a counterpart in the history of Western opera. It calls to mind the figure of the operatic castrato, the paradigmatic voice of the medium. Boys were castrated in order to produce a bizarre, marvellous, and deformed singing voice. Both the operatic voice and foot-binding blend beauty with cruelty, violence, and the erotic. Fundamental to the history of Western opera is the invention of a new aesthetic of beauty: An unnatural yet alluring voice, created by the castration of preadolescent boys. Its eroticism, emerging from an unnatural re-formation of the body, is similar to that of Chinese foot-binding, which inhibits the growth of girls' feet and deforms the foot into the shape of a flower. Castration is linked to the modification of the male voice and the enhancement of vocal powers in a manner analogous to the way the artificial moulding of a female foot creates erotic allure (for a similar view see Thomas, 1995).

Castrati

The castrato is an intentionally constructed voice, for whom the anatomy has artificially been altered: '[H]is voice was made—it was made by surgeons, singing masters, and the singers' (Gordon, 2015, p. 650). The castrati were castrated before puberty so that they would retain their high boy's voices. The voice of the castrato, unnaturally created, could not be matched by any natural voice. They were known for the beauty of their extraordinary timbre, their exceptional breath control, stamina, coloratura, tessitura, and incredible technique due to their famously uncompromising practice regimes.

There is scarce information about the process, but this is what we know:

> The anesthetic process–a combination of opium and bilateral carotid compression—led to significant morbidity and mortality. Aside from bilateral orchiectomy, there are also descriptions of atrophy via 'constant' compression and a method employing incandescent tongs to remove the entire scrotum and its contents.[8]

Around 4,000 boys were castrated annually in hopes of achieving operatic success. They came not only from poor economic backgrounds. Throughout the 17th and 18th centuries, the procedure was routine, even though the majority of castrated boys did not become successful singers. Prohibition against women's voices in the Church led to the use of boys, falsetti and castrati to sing the parts written for high voices. The fashion then moved to secular music, predominantly in Italy. Castration was used as a medical treatment for several maladies[9] and thus, at the time, was regarded differently than it is today (Heller, 2005, p. 307). It was, however, illegal: '[T]heir castration, forbidden under canon rule, was justified by the Church and society in terms of Catholic blood sacrifice' (Protz, 2015, p. 104). Castrati were popular from the late 16th to the late 18th centuries, spreading from Italy to other countries in Europe.[10] These castrated males in their operatic roles stood for God, the King, the ruler—they were idealized men. Their popularity declined in the 19th century as a result of new ethical codes and changes in operatic styles.

The relation between foot-binding and the castrato is not an explicit theme of the opera *The Empress's Feet*, but it becomes central to the performance of the opera, which I will now discuss.

Fold

All the themes outlined above come together in a production of *The Empress's Feet*, mounted under my direction in 2014, performed by my Tel Aviv–based ensemble TA OPERA ZUTA (TA OPERA ZUTA, 2014).[11]

The opera's stage design can be traced to themes related to foot-binding and sleepwalking. The practice of foot-binding involves folding the toes onto the inseam of the foot to form a lotus-like shape. Folding and unfolding are fundamental dimensions of the attraction of the image, of the flowering of the imagination. They are central to the conception of the opera's design—for the performance of *The Empress's Feet* seems at times to be the unfolding of a dream. The central static element of the design is a large, vertical, milky white plastic board, lit from the back, upon which are arranged and pasted 12 identical elements. Each of these elements is made out of a rectangle of plastic cloth, folded origami-like into a shape suggestive of a large foot (or shoe). Tacked onto the board, the elements, arranged in the form of a gate, suggest something like the entrance to a Chinese palace (see Image 2.1). The elements give a distinct sense of having been folded into this shape, not only because of the association with origami but also due to the lighting, which brings out clear distinctions among their dark shades and makes visible the differences in the layers of the folded shape.

The folded elements remain on the board throughout the opera until its last scene. During that scene, the elements are detached from the light-board and unfolded, and then spread out flat on the back of the board. The scene of unfolding and reconfiguring is lighted by reddish light that gradually turns white after the unfolding takes place and the elements are reconfigured into a new arrangement. Gradually, through lighting effects, the spread-out sheets form a red-coloured pattern suggesting two enormous feet. This is the only moment when colour is present in a design scheme that is predominantly white. It relates back to the voiceless tiny red shoes for bound feet shown at the outset of the

Image 2.1 The Empress's Feet. Gate made of elements folded in the form of a foot. Photographer: Tali Bøgen (Performer: Jonathan Opinya).

performance (discussed below), and suggests, within this fantasy, the violence required to produce castrati and lotus-shaped feet.

Soaring voice

For the single voice that must carry the entire weight of the piece, we cast an unnatural sounding timbre, a disembodied voice emerging from loudspeakers in surround sound. The staging portrays no evident correlations among sound, body, performer, voice, or word. The free-floating, unanchored recording is of a countertenor singer. This timbre repeatedly unsettles our sense of a singing body. Scholars have argued that, according to present-day knowledge, the countertenor is not a substitute for a castrato voice but rather represents a special category of its own (Demarco, 2002, pp. 174–5). Listeners, however, often conflate the voice of a countertenor with the castrato, or what is still more often than not believed to be that voice. Indeed, a countertenor sings in the extreme upper range of a natural male voice and is a relatively rare voice (Demarco, 2002, p. 174): 'The countertenor's vocal register and vocal production—that is, the use of falsetto with contemporary bel canto vocal production—create a truly unique sound, which has not existed heretofore in music history' (Fugate, 2016, p. 2).[12] The countertenor's voice approximates the quality and timbre of the female voice. It is often difficult for countertenors to sing loudly, as to do so would make their voices sound strained and forced. Casting a countertenor in the performance of TA OPERA ZUTA implicates opera, hinting toward the medium of opera's version, as it were, of bound feet: Castration of boys for aesthetic purposes. The performance re-inscribes the cruelty-beauty linkage of foot-binding present in the fairy tale, which is not explicit in the opera itself.

The performance provides no onstage performer to dispel or confirm what is heard from the loudspeakers. It takes the listener a while to figure out the terms of the work: A single voice carries all the weight; there are no clues to correlate sound, body, voice or word; levels of illusion are merged; a timbre that sounds like a woman's is that of a countertenor; the voice is not live but disembodied, emerging from loudspeakers in surround sound, free-floating and unanchored; a recording of a countertenor, standing in for a bygone voice, unsettles the sense of what can and cannot emanate from a body.

The performance's first gesture, before the sound of the countertenor's voice is heard, is established by storytelling. So that before the opera begins, a reading of the fairy tale—and by a bass voice—takes place. This gesture positions singing in relation to a narration of the fairy tale. It juxtaposes the fairy tale and the opera's modes of performativity, altering the perceptions of both speaking and singing. When he sings, doubling the recording, the bass voice opens up a wide gap with the countertenor's vocal range and timbre. The bass voice does not match the pace of the recording: At times the singer is in delay, at other times he lip-syncs. Rarely does the bass singer come to replace the pre-recorded voice. The deep, low voice is staged such that it seems to cause feet to move, as if it is of the feet. Since the work has no recourse to character but rather shifts among different modalities of memory, wakefulness and slumber, the audience does not perceive the opera's voices as emanating from characters and expressing their identities. The possibility opens up that the voices are heard as belonging to and emanating from the inanimate.

An additional short scene is inserted between the reading of the fairy tale and opera's singing. A small square area of the stage is illuminated, and within it are placed two tiny red slippers, sized for bound feet. The performers insert their hands into the slippers, making them into puppets. The slippers, enlivened, are manipulated like marionettes. The hands appear as though they are distorted feet inscribed in a beautiful object. The scene ends with the performers' feet, showing their size in relation to the minute slippers. The red shoes, in their miniaturization and distance, evoke sadness and desolation. Situated between speaking and singing but belonging to neither world, hovering. A voiceless object haunts the performance (Connor, 2014, p. 8).

Hollowed-out voice

At the same time, the performance makes figural the range of conditions of sleepwalking consciousness that are evoked in the opera, not restricting itself to the fairy tale source. The performance explores singing through its intimations of somnambulist consciousness. For sleepwalking is, precisely, a dissociation of behaviour from a person's presence of mind. It manifests itself in a body that performs separately from its unity with the soul that, in its normal state, is merely its other side. Because the state of sleepwalking cannot be recollected, and since one of its determining traits is amnesia about everything that happens during a sleepwalking episode, it is performed without awareness. A sleepwalker is someone who never tells a story; the body, as it were, takes over and performs that story.

In the fairy tale, the Empress's sleepwalking is kept secret, unwillingly brought to light only when the Emperor hears whispers. For him, whispering holds illicit thoughts, danger. Under the threat of beheading one of the servants, the whispers' contents are revealed. They disclose the sleepwalking. The opera turns whispering into an emblem of the sleepwalker's dreams or, more precisely, of the attempt to do away with sleepwalking. The whispers perform the suppression of sleepwalking.

There are two 'dream' scenes in the opera that call for the trying technique of whispering. The scenes are free, improvisatory and devoid of singing. They are the only scenes in the opera comprising texts without notated music. The dreams enact and at the same time fragmentarily and incomprehensively narrate the recurrence of sleepwalking episodes as nightmares (see Images 2.2–2.3). It is difficult to discern the sense of the text since it is low, hushed, hidden and delivered rapidly, the sentences disjointed and asyntactic. The stage directions call for a 'rapid' delivery, 'mostly unintelligible' and growing 'gradually more frantic'; when out of breath, the performer is to inhale the words. The stage directions form part of the improvisational whispered text that the performer is free to repeat and loop at will. The scenes are evocative yet obscure. One occurs prior to the operation and one takes place after it. The texts of the two scenes are nearly identical, as though the first dream prefigures the operation and the resulting loss of voice. Whispers, voiced on the verge of what one can hear, are clearly not intended for one's ears and may therefore contain terrible truths. In the opera, one imagines the whisper as a vibration communicated by the feet. It is the sound, the unvoiced voice or the acoustics of sleepwalking. Whispers are residues and faint echoes of the voice. The voice is thinned-out, composed of breaths. Hollowed out, the whispered voice sings its absence, inhaling and exhaling what little remains. The whisper scenes juxtapose text fragments that are on the threshold of the audible and comprehensible. They are breathless, frantic bad dreams. They sound the voiceless, the void, the ghostly. Though unvoiced and nearly impossible to understand, whispers obtain volume, duration and limited pitch; they can be made only with heavy aspiration, fortissimo, consonant projection and articulation. For the performer, whispering is fatiguing for the voice, and whispering poorly may cause the performer's voice to tire more easily: 'Since [the whisper] is unvocalized, air will escape faster and no natural resonance will be present in the sound. Whispered sounds cannot be sustained as long as sung

Image 2.2 The Empress's Feet. Dreamlike sleepwalking scene. Photographer: Tali Bøgen (Performers: Goni Paz and Ofri Omer).

Image 2.3 The Empress's Feet. Dreamlike sleepwalking scene. Photographer: Tali Bøgen (Performers: Goni Paz, Ofri Omer, and Jonathan Opinya).

tones because of this. Therefore, more frequent breaths will be needed' (Mabry, 2002, p. 128–9).

Steven Connor regards the soft low murmur, the whisper, to be a sketch or outline of the voice. We are 'uncertain whether it belongs to the inside or the outside, the whisper is always also scattered, with no fixed abode.' (Connor, 2014, p. 49). A whisper, he continues, is 'voice-less,' 'spectre-speaking', and 'entirely nocturnal' (Connor, 2014, p. 48); 'it gives us too little, that the almost-but-not-quite nothing of the voice-that-is-not-one thereby craves from us the making of a voice-body of compensatory density and intensity. Perhaps all whispers are kin to the shades of the underworld' (Connor, 2014, p. 51). Connor relates whispering to one of the ways that ventriloquism was understood:

speaking through the body from some place, or by some means, other than the mouth, and therefore as an improper or displaced form of speaking which might then appear to be coming from elsewhere, and so to be magical or devilish. The whisper is this voice, embodied, but without abode.

(Connor, 2014, p. 50)

It is 'a kind of feigning or counterfeiting out of which all colour, body and melody have been drained' (Connor, 2014, p. 51). As voice drained of melody and timbre, the whisper assumes the position of other to singing. Hovering on the brink of perception, the whisper belongs to the realm of shadows, to the construction of sleepwalking as terrifying. Whispers depend on the voice for signification as unvoiced and unsung, not telling of but enacting somnambulism.

Ficarra and Whittington reposition and redefine whispering: They do not disclose but embody the secret of nocturnal walks and at the same time manifest the attempt to suppress them. The whisper becomes the resonance of the night, voicing the refusal to stop sleepwalking. Whispers, speaking through the body, displace singing about the body. The performance tells of the knowledge that belongs to sleepwalking, to an altered mode of awareness by voicing the body, its motion, trajectory and wishes dissociated from consciousness.

One whisper scene I staged as an illusion of feet, sovereign and aerial, walking themselves. Light is projected solely on the feet as an acrobat walks in empty darkness. The pace of her steps is her own, as opposed to movement in other scenes that is governed by the music. A sense of the divided consciousness of sleepwalking is figured in the dissociation between the surrounding humming and her walking. Her airy sleepwalk is puppeteered, as she is pulled and pushed by cables manoeuvred by the performers. Marionette-like, she is unaffected by gravity. A 'flying' nocturnal creature, feet-walked in isolation from the acoustic surroundings (see Image 2.4).

In the other whisper scene, a tiny prop held in the performers' hands—a flat, miniature, two-dimensional folded sheet of origami paper—stands in for feet. The listener is led to perceive the whispers as emanating from this prop. This displaced surrogate foot is a music box without a resonance chamber, sounding unvoiced.

Aerial acrobat

Singing becomes the imagination of a different register, of knowledge of, through and by the body. The sleepwalker, a 'flying soul', a 'sleep virtuoso', possesses secret ways to move. Sleepwalking is evoked in a staging in which the feet induce and lead movement. The body is animated; the pace is of breathing, associating movement during sleep

Image 2.4 The Empress's Feet. Feet walking in mid-air. Photographer: Tali
    Bøgen (Performer: Reenat Caidar Avraham).

with the work's vocal effect of whispering. The performance blurs any
distinction between movement initiated from within the body, as it
were, and movement prompted by what lies outside it. Like puppets
and puppeteers, sleep and wakefulness (see Image 2.5).

These moves are figured in the performance by the aerial acrobat,
for whom the feet are strong, bound high and admired for their virtuosity and the possibilities of movement they can satisfy. An acrobat's
performance is at odds with what regulates everyday bodily encounters and defines their conformity; the performer's movements and oc-
cupation of space are often at odds with the register of regular human
capacities. Here is a body that counters the pull of gravity that governs our dealings with the world while awake. Neither anchored to the
ground nor fixed in a position in space, an acrobat may roam space,
aerial-like, float, soar above the audience's heads. An acrobatic act
destabilizes equilibrium and defies nature's laws. A fearless body, un-
defeatable, unlimited, repeatedly taking risks. A death-defying body:

'An acrobat increases and accentuates the difference between his
behavior and the norm [...] The spectator [...] considers the acrobat

Image 2.5 The Empress's Feet. Sleep totem. Photographer: Tali Bøgen (Performers: Goni Paz, Ofri Omer, and Reenat Caidar Avraham).

"another sort" of being' (Bouissac, 1985, p. 45). Not restricted by weight or by a necessary stability or balance, an acrobat seems to walk itself, as if it really were some sort of somnambulistic 'flying soul.' An acrobat maintains an illusion of physical freedom, with the feet seeming unrestrained, going forth on their own accord, elevating the body high above, airborne, in display, in excessive use. As if really given agency. The body in the air, carried by the feet, transport the Empress farther away.

In TA OPERA ZUTA's staging of the opera, foot-binding is implicated in the analogy with the castrato via its most common stand-in, the voice of the countertenor. In turn, voice is established as that which emanates from a sleepwalker's consciousness, staged by way of acrobatic feet. Together, the virtuosic feet that walk in the air and an all-governing, odd, high voice seem hallucinatory to us. As if the body in the air itself had no weight, were non-material, a figment of the imagination, for which the countertenor's voice acts as material manifestation:

> The voice goes out from the body as the body's twin—as a body double. [...] The voice is the body's second life, something between

a substance and a force—a fluency that is yet a form. The voice is lived and imagined as the life of its subject. [...] [Voice is] imagined to have the power to radiate new life back to the body from which it emanates.

(Connor, 2014, pp. 17–8)

Notes

1 A shorter and diverse version of this chapter appears as 'Voice and the sleepwalking body', *Theatre Research International*, 46(2), 2021, pp. 128–147
2 On the composer see Ficarra, 2017. On the librettist see Whittington, 2020.
3 We are in the realm of the Little Mermaid, who earns her human feet while in pain and at the price of the loss of her voice, and of Cinderella, who possesses the smallest foot in the land, the one that makes the perfect match with the shoe. The latter tale originated in China in the 9th century—around the time of the origin of the custom of foot-binding. Susanne Sara Thomas (1995) terms the foot that perfectly fits the shoe a 'phallic foot'. Fitting the shoe is the climax of the tale, and stands for the sexual act. She argues that foot-binding renders the foot phallic. For the symbol of the shoe in fertility rituals and marriage and as forms of possession see Nacht, 1915.
4 'The similarity of the process in the emergence of the spirit world and the analogy between the forces prevailing in the inner life with the magnetic state (excursus on magnetism, the gradations of magnetic sleep etc.)' (Schelling, 2000, pp. 65–72).
5 The two sleepwalking scenes share a form of secrecy with *The Empress's Feet*. Lady Macbeth's gestures of erasure act out her secret acts. For Amina and the Empress the fact of sleepwalking is the secret.
6 See for instance: Patricia Buckley Ebrey, 'Gender and sinology: Shifting western interpretations of footbinding, 1300–1890', *Women and the family in Chinese history* (London: Routledge, 2003), pp. 194–219.
7 Kristeva's view is criticized by Chow, 1997, pp. 6–7.
8 Hennessey and Harnisch, 2019. And further: 'Prepubertal androgen deprivation prevents vocal cord elongation and thickening, allowing for both a higher vocal range and more nimble, delicate ornamentation. Additionally, low testosterone levels can delay epiphyseal closure, which led to unusually large ribcages and unrivalled lung power'. See also Gordon, 2015, p. 651:

> Castrati had higher voices and extra brilliance that came from the short, thin vocal cords and the close proximity of the larynx to the head. Famous for the vocal pyrotechnics, vocal control, and brilliance of tone enabled by the castration procedure, they also had bodies that stood out as unusual. The alterity of every part of their physicality highlights the madness of the voice and the similitude between the stuff of the body and the stuff of the voice. Boys who were castrated lost the major source of testosterone before puberty. For the purposes of singing, this meant that their larynxes stayed small and did not descend into the throat. They had the vocal box of prepubescent boys. But they also often developed extra large chests, heads, jaws, and noses, which meant that their resonating chambers were much larger

in proportion to their vocal materials than in unaltered bodies. Lack of testosterone meant that growth plates in the joints did not fuse at the normal time, and often their limbs, jaws, facial bones, and ribs grew to extraordinary length, giving them a strange appearance. They had flat feet, never grew beards, had luxuriant hair on their scalps, developed extra fat deposits on their chests and hips, and tended toward obesity later in life.

9 'Though canon law had long forbidden bodily mutilation, castration was thought to cure a variety of ailments including epilepsy, gout, and hernia. It also served as a form of corporal punishment' (Gordon, 2015, p. 652).

10 See Feldman, 2015, Chapter 5, for a new explanation of the decline of the castrati in late 18th century.

11 TA OPERA ZUTA (2014) Performance of *The Empress's Feet*, Tmuna Theatre, Tel Aviv, Israel. Available on my wepage michalgroverfriedlander.com/performances/theempressfeet-ficarra-whittington-2014.
  Singing (recording): Doron Schleifer. **Performance Artists:** Jonathan Opinya, Ofri Omer, Gony Paz, Reenat Caidar Avraham. **Directing and Artistic Management:** Michal Grover-Friedlander. **Stage Design and Props:** Eli Friedlander, Thom Friedlander, Coline Faucon. **Lighting and Sound Design:** Nadav Barnea. **Production:** Shira Yasur.

12 Another important distinction alluded to by Fugate is that between countertenors in different singing styles:

> Hard rock singers produce falsetto sounds that are powerful, strained, tense, and piercing, which is often interpreted as masculine in the stereotypical Western mindset. Soul/R&B singers use a more intimate falsetto and, in comparison, could seem less masculine/more feminine. So, the production of sound affects the perception of the listener. As aforementioned, the capacity of bel canto technique to create loud or resonant sounds could influence the perception of the listener to the extent that a high-pitched falsetto voice can sound very masculine.
>
> (Fugate, 2016, p. 119)

For distinction between countertenor and falsetto, Fugate also remarks:

> Making distinctions between the early sound of the male falsettist and that of the contemporary countertenor is very important due to the fact that the countertenor, who utilizes bel canto singing techniques as opposed to pop/folk singing styles, possesses a very unique sound in the history of Western singing.
>
> (Fugate, 2016, p. 16)

3 Staging thought in Satie's *Socrate* (1919)

Of the three stagings discussed in this book, the staging of Satie's *Socrate* demanded from me the most extensive process of preparatory study. I explored aspects of the piece's genesis; its compositional context, such as Satie's idea of *furniture music*; *Socrate*'s exceptional reception—in which major visual artists reframed and recreated the work in other media; Satie's overall musical aesthetics; the figure of Socrates, the legendary philosopher; the Platonic texts Satie chose to include and exclude, as well as interpretations of themes found in these texts. In this chapter, more so than in previous chapters, a lengthy presentation is necessary before embarking on the actual staging. As with the prior chapter, I will nevertheless provide some preliminary orientation.

What would be music for thought? What is the singing voice of thought? These are questions that I asked myself when turning to an opera that puts into music the figure of the ultimate teacher of philosophy, Socrates, an opera whose text is drawn from excerpts from Plato's dialogues. For sure, much has been written about consigning Socrates originally face-to-face dialogic interactions to written form. But the live performance of Plato's text, set to music, is a whole different matter.

Thought in its purity would dwell in the intelligible realm of ideas, as it were, entirely lacking a body. And supposedly, after death, when the soul leaves the body, it fulfils its ultimate inner telos (unless it were to return to another body via metempsychosis, which, in Plato's worldview, is the punishment of those who lived badly). Can music, or singing, be that ethereal body or evanescent material presenting the figure of the philosopher who cheerfully accepts such death? One way is by suggesting the bodily or material quality of the singing voice. But how to stage and express this relation of music and matter?

DOI: 10.4324/9781003187257-4

The set is a material presence so that the voice may reveal itself to be one with that materiality. This mode of staging the voice is what I call in the introduction *visual staging*. By this I mean that voice and music seem to echo the visual elements making up the staging. In *Socrate* the set is minimal and almost monochromatic, analogous to the music of Satie. The set consisted of gradations of white, different shades, transparent and opaque. Most importantly, the set brings matter to the fore: glass, clear water, turbid, milky water, white wax, yellow wax, honey. The elements of the set can be seen as variants of one another, resonating with the musical logic and compositional technique employed by Satie.

Matter seems to be in attunement with the music as a garland of paper unfolds in the water, in a natural process that matches exactly the rhythm of singing. Liquid wax poured into the water becomes opaque, hard, resistant and brittle as the soul leaves the body with a last breath of song, solidifying into Socrates's death mask.

But we would not be dealing with Socrates, were the question not raised of the tense relation of music, of art, to thought, even if a horizon of their reconciliation remains in view. That tense co-existence is, as will become clear, a major factor in Satie's choice as to which parts of the dialogues to set to music. Yet the singing voice must also appear as a disturbance of pure thought. Beyond the thematic elaborations, which I will discuss in what follows, I wish to mention at the outset one moment of the staging which attempted to exhibit singing as an obstacle, as a self-contained moment in the mode of what I call *vocal disturbance*. Inserted into the work at the moment when Socrates speaks of the beauty of the swan song as the swan nears its death, I intercalated a Renaissance madrigal. Not only is the melancholy death of the bird in music set in opposition to Socrates's image of the swan song. The madrigal is staged so that sound itself is foregrounded—one is acutely aware of the stylistic features of the music, the way the music is sung and so forth—so as to give the sense of a self-referential, self-enclosed moment. The experience is deliberately and manifestly embedded in nothing other than sound and its material presence. The moment is staged so as to form a self-contained loop of song, repeating the madrigal until its end in a distorted rendering of it on a toy piano.

Enigmatic work

Socrate is considered by many to be Erik Satie's most moving, serious, and important music. Some scholars see it as a landmark in the evolution of neoclassicism. However, it is a curious and enigmatic piece, difficult to contextualize and to comprehend, as Pietro Dossena (2008, pp. 3–4) claims:

> *Socrate* seems to possess something peculiar—many critics underline its uniqueness, both in Satie's oeuvre and in the history of music—and it is certainly a problematic piece, atypical, and impossible to pigeonhole... For critics this has led to disorientation coupled with fascination. Even today *Socrate* remains impenetrable and enigmatic.

Some listeners hear in *Socrate* yet another of Satie's ironic works. The subtitle *Symphonic Drama in Three Parts with Voice* indeed rings ironic to scholars: '*Socrate* is by no means symphonic in a traditional sense, as there is no conventional development of material, and the size of the orchestra is small. Neither is it properly dramatic, as there is no represented action.' Having the text drawn from the Socratic dialogues also contributes to this impression. Is Satie being ironic? Is Socratic irony invoked?[1] As for contemporary critics, their reactions were mixed. Expecting Satie's typically parodic, provocative witty style, the work's early listeners were perplexed, highly critical and dismissive: 'I was sorry for the singer, who had to rush through the dialogues of Plato in a dreary recitative, without variety, without tunefulness, without punctuation, or declamatory emphasis [...] everybody seemed bored and wondered when it would all finish' (quoted in Gillmor, 1988, p. 218). Other critics, though, were fascinated by *Socrate* and were taken by its seriousness: 'All the emotion of the admirable text was expressed with nobility, discretion, and the most perfect purity' (quoted in Gillmor, 1988, p. 218).

Flexible timbre

Princess Edmond de Polignac was a musical patron who commissioned *Socrate* from Satie. She also commissioned works from Stravinsky, Milhaud, Poulenc, and Weill. Together with her husband, the princess established one of the central salons of the artistic and musical avant-garde in Paris between the two world wars. The salon hosted several important first performances. The hostess served as patron to artists and performers, among them Nadia Boulanger, Clara Haskil, Arthur Rubinstein, Vladimir Horowitz, Ethel Smyth, Le Corbusier, and the Ballets Russes. Numerous famous artists and intellectuals of the time frequented the salon: Proust, Isadora Duncan, Cocteau, Monet, Diaghilev, and Colette.

The princess intended to perform *Socrate* herself with two of her women friends. She envisioned a kind of melodrama, with the philosophical text in the original Greek recited by women to Satie's background music. The commission from Satie was to be performed in her salon along with Stravinsky's *Renard*, also commissioned by the princess, as both were to be scored for a small ensemble of 16 players.[2]

It was Polignac's idea to concentrate on the death of Socrates as depicted in Plato's *Phaedo*. Information is scant about what went on between the time of this inaugural idea and the finished work, completed around a year and a half later. Satie's initial idea was along the lines of the princess's conception: The music was to be in the background as the princess and two of her female friends, seated in armchairs, recited from Plato in Greek. Aspects of the initial concept—'background', 'armchair', 'recitation'—remained important for Satie, as I show below, in relation to his notion of *furniture music*. In the final version, the text of *Socrate* is in French, not in Greek (using Victor Cousin's somewhat out-of-date translations). Satie's *Socrate* ultimately comprises three parts, each based on a different dialogue; only the final of the three parts relates Socrates's death and, accordingly, is based on *Phaedo*, while the two other parts are based on *Symposium* and *Phaedrus*. In his correspondence, Satie refers to his work as 'The Life of Socrates' [*La vie de Socrate*] and 'Socrate', rather than 'Death of Socrates', as the project grew from a death scene into a kind of portrait.

Sopranos and mezzo-sopranos are cast to sing the roles of Socrates and his interlocutors. It is left open whether one, two, three or four female singers are to perform the vocal part(s). Narration and all direct speech are undifferentiated vocally. Indeed, early performance accounts attest to great flexibility in terms of timbre, vocal as well as instrumental: There was a plan to execute the work with a children's chorus (such a performance did not materialize) and a performance with André Gide reciting the vocal part; there was also Satie's refusal to grant the celebrated actor Pierre Bertin permission to perform the work[3]; and the first public stagings (1920) were given with two singers and piano and with singer and orchestra.

Satie's Plato

Satie's treatment of text does not serve as a straightforward guide to the work.[4] This is also true for *Socrate*: A good deal of text is deployed and it is all consciously comprehensive—it is in recitative, is syllabic, is equally accented and is predominantly in conjunct motion—and for all these reasons it is very clear. Satie chooses three of Plato's most famous and important dialogues, *Symposium*, *Phaedrus*, and *Phaedo*, and correspondingly he divides the composition into three parts: 'Portrait of Socrates', 'On the Banks of the Ilissus', and the longest and final part, 'Death of Socrates'. The composer worked meticulously with the text. He takes few sections, between two and four, and they are often non-consecutive; at first glance, at least in the first two parts, these choices are perplexing. The music simply does not change in relation to the words. The music neither illustrates words nor accentuates or contradicts them:

> Music carefully avoids seeming to have any relationship whatsoever to the words. Music seems to accept not taking account of Plato's text as its duty...
>
> (Jankélévitch, 2003, pp. 45–6, 48)

What Vladimir Jankélévitch is in fact saying about *Socrate* here is that the music is not a setting of Plato's text.

I would characterize the text Satie has chosen in three ways. First, it is not primarily made up of philosophical dialogue. Second, it refers to music. Third, it does not take up some of the most striking accounts of music that can be found elsewhere in Plato.[5]

To elaborate: The first part is a drunken rejected lover's account of the philosopher, and the second part paints a scene of repose for the onset of philosophical conversation—but not the discussion itself. Only the third part, the longest textual excerpt, concerns Socrates approaching his death and features some lines about the immortality of the soul. But I would claim that a closer look reveals the hidden common theme behind these selections. The first part conveys the seductive force of Socrates's voice and his talk via musical imagery. Socrates is figured as a hybrid creature, situated somewhere between the animal and the divine: His voice is seductive as the sirens', his speech more powerful than the enchanting music of the satyr Marsyas. The second part depicts scenery, placing the philosopher within a set.[6] Philosophical conversation is positioned in opposition to the background sounds of nature: The singing of cicadas. This sound is tempting and thus threatens the very act of philosophizing.[7] The final part portrays one of the significant cultural legacies of Socrates: His attitude towards death. The philosopher reflects on death by way of the swan's death song. Philosophy yearns for the knowledge possessed by the swan's prophetic singing. Through the entire work the common theme underlying Satie's portrait of Socrates is, quite surprisingly, music.

Let us examine the first part in some detail, as it exemplifies the treatment of the philosophical source. Below is the full excerpt that the composer extracted from *Symposium* to form the first part, 'Portrait of Socrates':

> ALCIBIADES: And now, my boys, I shall praise Socrates in a figure which will appear to him to be a caricature, and yet I speak, not to make fun of him, but only for the truth's sake. I say, that he is exactly like the busts of Silenus, which are set up in the statuaries' shops, holding pipes and flutes in their mouths; and they are made to open in the middle, and have images of gods inside them. I say also that he is like Marsyas the satyr. [...] And are you not a flute-player? That you are, and a performer far more wonderful than Marsyas. He indeed with instruments used to charm the souls of men by the power of his breath, and the players of his music do so still: for the melodies of Olympus are derived from Marsyas who taught them [...] But you produce the same effect with your words only, and do not require the flute: that is the difference between you and him. [...] And if I were not afraid that you would think me hopelessly drunk, I would have sworn as well as spoken to the influence which they have always had and still have over me. For my heart leaps within me more than that of any Corybantian reveler, and my eyes rain tears when I hear them. And I observe that many others are affected in the same manner. [...] And this is what I and many others have suffered from the flute-playing of this satyr.
>
> SOCRATES: [...] you praised me, and I in turn ought to praise my neighbor on the right [...]
>
> (Symposium, 32–33–35)

The short excerpt abounds in words related to music, such as performer, melody, player of music; the word *flute* appears four times in the passage. Socrates is likened to two wind players. The first reference alludes to the busts of Silenus that hold pipes and flutes in their mouths. The wind instruments are on the exterior of the statues and are identified with Socrates's monstrous ugliness and repulsive exterior appearance rather than with the secret beauty and divine marvels residing within him. The second is Marsyas, the wondrous aulos player, the converter and charmer of souls. The philosopher's talk is equated with playing music—though Socrates's effect is greater and far more damaging than music's. It subjugates, brings about suffering, people are beside themselves because of it, tears flow, hearts leap, one wishes only for death. Marsyas's musicality is an act of hubris against the gods: His excessiveness, transgression and virtuosity end very badly. Indeed the music-related images are fundamentally problematic.

Alcibiades begins his praise of Socrates with a disclaimer that it might sound ironic, humorous, and degrading to the audience. The suspicion that the praise is un-truthful has some basis if we take into account Alcibiades's drunken entrance and his emotional state.[8] His perspective is of a jealous and rejected lover.

Satie does not include the speeches in praise of love that constitute the drinking party of *Symposium*, whose six members each in turn examine the genesis, purpose and nature of Eros. Neither does Satie provide us with Socrates's two speeches which are the high point of *Symposium*—where Socrates ascertains that the highest mode and the purpose of love is the love of wisdom, which represents the philosopher's highest aspiration.

Marsyas

The analogy with Marsyas, the satyr who plays the aulos so marvellously, is intriguing in relation to Socrates. We are told that Socrates's speech is compared to—indeed exceeds—Marsyas's enchanting playing. What that means is that the philosopher is associated with a musician and, moreover, to a defeated one, even one who suffered the god Apollo's cruel retribution.

The myth lurking beneath the surface of this analogy is the musical contest between Apollo and the satyr Marsyas. Apollo, Socrates's revered god, guardian of the Muses, god of light and the embodiment of proportion and harmony, plays the lyre; Marsyas, half-goat and half-man, visceral and sexually driven, an enchanting musician, plays the double-piped reed aulos. Marsyas finds the aulos after its inventor, the goddess of wisdom Athena, had discarded it because it deforms her face while she plays it, making her look unintelligent. The very origin of the instrument is in opposition to what Socrates stands for. The musical contest is set between one who is below and one who is above humankind. The satyr Marsyas dares to challenge the god Apollo to a musical competition, the terms being that the winner can treat the loser in any way he wishes. Some versions of the myth accord Marsyas victory after the first round, but when Apollo, turning his lyre upside down, plays the same tune—something Marsyas cannot do on his wind instrument—he loses, defeated by the god's trick. In other versions, Marsyas suffers defeat when Apollo sings to the sound of the lyre, again something that the satyr cannot do on a wind instrument. In all versions, Marsyas loses due to a ruse of Apollo's, and the victorious god orders that Marsyas be flayed alive. Enchanting music does not guarantee Marsyas's life, just as words do not guarantee Socrates's.

The myth does not end there. The dead satyr's suspended skin becomes a bag containing wind, and when the winds blow, it swells into the shape of the satyr's body and produces music. As with an Aeolian harp, music is produced without a player. Or better, the player has lent his bodily shape to form a musical instrument. The skin of the dead musician is played upon by nature. The musician, in death, has become the instrument and the music. It is an instrument with ears: To the sound of music associated with Apollo, the skin keeps silent, refusing its music to the retributive god's agents. Not unlike Orpheus' decapitated head that sings, Marsyas, hollowed-out, resonates in the wind. Yet unlike Orpheus, Marsyas neither sings nor plays a string instrument—he is equivocated between two polar opposite gods, Dionysus and Apollo (see Mellers, 1987, p. 1).

As Steven Connor interprets it, the story of the contest between Apollo and Marsyas enacts competing theories about the production of voice. Early anatomists possessed two competing theories to explain the structure and function of the larynx. One saw the voice as a wind instrument, akin to reed, flute or organ pipe; the other regarded the voice as a stringed instrument. The voice was a wind instrument in that it employed air, but the modulation of strings or cords produced a stringed instrument in sound. The voice could therefore be seen as a kind of Aeolian harp, its strings sounded by the inner breeze of the breath. The voice as a stringed instrument partook in the rational intervals of the Apollonian lyre; the voice as a wind instrument was closer to the respiring and expiring human body (Connor, 2004).

Apollo and Marsyas stand for opposite conceptions of musical experience. Marsyas stands for music (in the Greek sense of word, tone, movement) that 'threatens to turn you into something you are not' (Hamilton, 2013, pp. 35–48). Marsyas, with his insatiable sexual appetite, is the figure of excess. He breaks through limitations and definitions. He is the expression of music as immediate and evanescent. Thus Marsyas's aulos stands for an ability to express oneself so powerfully and immediately that the satyr could believe he'd outdo a god, that he could communicate the contents of his soul directly, without mediation—uncontaminated, formless and without speech. The aulos is closer than the lyre to the human voice and pure sound; it is the excess of breath and is associated with drunkenness and the irrational. Marsyas is in a position of protest against language's exclusive claim to the production of meaning; he stands against language's objectification and transformation of an instant into an idea. Marsyas's music is sound, not a sign or symbol of signification. It is a material substance. It is the position of the present, of being-in-the-moment.[9] Whereas Apollo expresses music as an idea: Meditation, transcendence and form. The lyre accompanies the song's words and is calm and logical, showing words to control music. These matters, however, are not so clearly contrasted if we consider the story of Silenus. Silenus possesses great wisdom, but his sagacity is revealed only under duress. Silenus is a seer, and his wisdom lies in singing, in revealing, when captured, the secrets of nature. Two shepherds, coming upon Silenus drunk and asleep, bind him in the hopes of redeeming an unfulfilled promise of song. Silenus, in song, both communicates knowledge and enchants. He is an expression of both gods.[10]

Cicadas

Socrate's second part, 'On the banks of the Ilissus', is also brief, using two sections (4–5) of Plato's *Phaedrus*. Phaedrus and Socrates are taking a walk outside the city gates of Athens, looking for a quiet spot to sit down and converse. They reach a resting place, where the sensations, sounds and scents of summer abound: A spreading plane tree in fullest blossom and fragrance, grass, a flowing stream deliciously cool to the feet, and a sweet breeze. In the background, there are sounds that echo the ever-present chorus of cicadas. The spot spurs a discussion between Phaedrus and Socrates about the possibility of a rational accounting instead of the myth explicating the spot. It is a scene of sensations. Sight, smell, touch, and sound set the stage for a philosophical conversation. The sound provides a constant background, threatening to lull them, displease the Muses and undermine the purpose of the stroll: To philosophize.

In the background of the chirping insects lies a myth about the ever-present sound of the chorus of cicadas. The cicadas had originally been humans. When the Muses brought song into the world, they took such immense pleasure in singing that they forgot to eat, drink, and sleep, and sang themselves to death. The Muses rewarded their love of singing by turning them into cicadas, which never need food or sleep and sing from birth to death. The cicadas then become the Muses' messengers. They engage in spying, watching to see whether their music derails human conduct or is resisted. They then report back to the Muses with an account of who among the humans has honoured them. The cicadas' periodic lifecycle, emergence from the ground and metamorphosis stood for resurrection; their never-ceasing sound, for immortality. If, in the first part, Marsyas stands for music sounding beyond the confines of a living body and for music sounding the remains of the living, then, in the second part, cicadas denote unceasing song and the centrality of the pleasure of singing to the afterlife of humans.

Swan song

Socrates's death scene, undoubtedly one of the most famous deaths in Western culture, forms the third part of Satie's work. It presents Socrates's outlook on death and immortality as his own death approaches. *Phaedo*, the dialogue from which the death scene is extracted, is devoted to proving the existence of the afterlife. The death of the body sets the soul free, releasing the immortal soul from the bonds of a contingent body. Socrates's transition from life to death is the beatitude of the one who feels fully released from the call of the body and its attempt to control the soul. The true philosopher can escape the cycle of reincarnation visited upon most individuals and thus never again be imprisoned within a body. Socrates's peaceful death is a depiction of its meaning. Death is a philosophical idea, it is the very embodiment of a life devoted to philosophy. Philosophy is training for one's death.[11]

Satie's third part, 'Death of Socrates', includes the instructions for drinking the poison, an account of what Socrates is expected to feel, the drinking of the poison, the venom working its way through the body, and then, most importantly, Socrates's calm and joyful approach to his passing away,[12] likened to the swan's. When perceiving it is about to die, the bird, rejoicing in its approaching death, sings more beautifully than ever. The image of the swan echoes Socrates's account of the winged, immortal soul. Before the soul had been incarnated in a corporeal body it had dwelled among the divinities, had experienced their sublime beauty. When the soul entered the physical world and received a body, it forgot those sights. But whenever the soul finds beauty in another being, it senses a dim memory of the sights it had once seen, and this fills the soul with passionate love for that being. This love stems from the longing for divine beauty and the wish to merge with it. The wings of the soul spread as a manifestation of passion and become the means of spiritual transcendence and of the merging with the divine.

In ancient literature, a swan's final song possessed a double meaning. On the one hand, it was understood as festive, as in Socrates's account. It celebrated communion with god after death. On the other hand, it was heard as a lament for passing away. In music, the meaning of the swan's death song as lament has prevailed. Satie, however, does not incorporate this meaning of the swan song, even though it is present in Socrates's speech in the *Phaedo*:

> But men, because they are themselves afraid of death, slanderously affirm of the swans that they sing a lament at the last, not considering that no bird sings when cold, or hungry, or in pain, not even the nightingale, nor the swallow, nor yet the hoopoe; which are said indeed to tune a lay of sorrow, although I do not believe this to be true of them any more than of the swans. But because they are sacred to Apollo, they have the gift of prophecy, and anticipate the good things of another world, wherefore they sing and rejoice in that day more than they ever did before. And I too, believing myself to be the consecrated servant of the same God, and the fellow-servant of the swans, and thinking that I have received from my master gifts of prophecy which are not inferior to theirs, would not go out of life less merrily than the swans.
>
> [85b]

Satie might be attracted to the meaning that links the swan to Apollo, and not only in its joyful attitude towards death: The swan is known to be Apollo's sacred and prophetic singer, and Apollo travels on a chariot of swans. Moreover, the swan figures in the myth about the invention of the lyre. Apollo is said to have bound seven strings to his lyre, matching the number of times that swans circled the delivery bed in flight, singing over his birth pains.[13] The swan figures in the myth about Apollo's discovery of the octave in that it is believed that the swan sings the span of an octave.[14]

These myths reverberate forcefully beneath the surface of Satie's accentuated imagery. They situate the philosopher within a Dionysian-Apollonian orbit comprising enchanting music, music-playing gods, the Muses' gifts.

'One becomes more of a philosopher the more one becomes a musician': Nietzsche's Socrates[15]

In Nietzsche's famous indictment of Socrates in his *Birth of Tragedy*, he blames the Socratic spirit for bringing death upon the tragic spirit. For if the core of tragedy is, according to Nietzsche, musical, Socrates is viewed as the man who brought about the death of tragedy. He is seen as having a wholly unmusical sensibility. Indeed, Nietzsche's *Birth of*

Tragedy calls for the rebirth of tragedy as the metaphysical art that can shape the destiny of humanity to come. Initially, Nietzsche identifies this rebirth of a tragedy out of music and the overcoming of artistic Socratism in the musical character of Wagnerian musical drama. By contrast, he identifies Socratism in music with the *stilo rappresentativo* of Baroque opera, a style that ignores and distorts the essence of music since it follows the words it is paired with. That is, music is subordinated to the meaning conveyed by words rather than the meaning that emerges from attributes of music as such. Thus music is not conceived as constituting a womb of the visible world and its happenings, out of which unity the drama is generated, but rather is seen as a mere emotional colouring of an already articulated meaning.

In this context, one might raise the question of whether there exists another sort of Socratic musical sensibility: That is, Socrates conceived as a principle not inimical to true art. Nietzsche himself was not as dismissive of this possibility as might first appear based on his attack on Socrates in *The Birth of Tragedy*.

Nietzsche, wondering about Socrates's erotic power, compares the philosopher's spellbinding effect on the youth of Athens to that of the pied piper on the mice of the town of Hamelin, according to the well-known medieval legend. This comparison is a further reference to a wind instrument in connection with Socrates's mastery of Eros. It suggests a connection to the passage from *Symposium* forming the basis of the first part of Satie's work, where Alcibiades identifies Socrates's power with that of the satyr Marsyas. The satyrs were companions of Dionysus. Such an identification challenges the view that Socrates has a purely Apollonian sensibility. Alcibiades's testimony about Socrates's seductive power might be proof that he has a hidden Dionysian side of which even he is not aware or which is still a potentiality for him. Indeed, at one point in *The Birth of Tragedy*, Nietzsche raises this notion as a latent possibility:

> And so, while it's true that the immediate effect of the Socratic drive was to bring about the destruction of Dionysian tragedy, the profound living experiences of Socrates himself force us to question whether or not there must necessarily be only an antithetical relationship between Socrates's doctrines and art, and whether the birth of an 'artistic Socrates' is in general something of a contradiction.

It is in *Phaedo*, in the account of the death of Socrates, that Nietzsche finds an unrealized possibility in Socrates's life hinted at, namely the possibility of a musical Socrates. On the eve of his execution, Socrates tells how his daemon told him that he should practice music. The philosopher wonders whether he has missed his true vocation:

> Frequently the same dream came to me, appearing at different times in different visages, but saying the same thing: 'Socrates, make music and practice it'. And I, in the past, assumed I was doing the very thing that they were exhorting and ordering me to do. Just like those men who urge on runners, so the dream was ordering me to do the very thing I was doing, namely making music, because philosophy is the greatest music and I was doing it. But now, [since the verdict came in and the festival of the god delayed my dying,] it seemed necessary, in case the dream was perhaps ordering me to make music in the ordinary sense (dhm≈dh), not to disobey it but to make it.

This quite strange and wonderful tale is central for Nietzsche, who was engrossed by the figure of Socrates. For Nietzsche, it shows cracks in the rational Socrates and points to Dionysian aspects alongside the Apollonian. Nietzsche projects his dream of reconciliation of Apollo and Dionysus into the image of Socrates the musician. Having answered the call to devote himself to music, Socrates, the musician, would then reconcile rational thought with daemonic enthusiasm. This image of Socrates is related to Nietzsche's account of music as Dionysian, and the image of Socrates as satyr—for satyrs are those creatures that accompany Dionysus and make up the chorus: The origin of tragedy as music.

The stakes are high for Nietzsche when he musicalizes Socrates. Satie, for his part, might not have immersed himself in Nietzsche's writings.[16] Indeed, the music-practicing Socrates from *Phaedo* is not something Satie incorporates into his portrait. And yet, there is nonetheless an affinity here, as Satie's Socrates re-emerges from the ashes of music, from the afterlife of singing.

White

In a letter from the time of the composition of *Socrate*, Satie writes: 'I'm scared of failing with this work, which I want to be white and pure like the Antique' (Satie, letter to Valentine Gross, 6 January 1917, Satie, 2000, p. 274). He also recounts that to get into the right mood as he was composing the piece he ate nothing but white foods. The juxtaposition of these two vignettes clearly brings out the enigma of the whiteness of Satie's *Socrate*. What would a 'white' composition be? Would the whiteness of the piece be a reference to classical Greece? Would it be an association to the whiteness of classical sculpture (which, one should note, had originally been coloured)? Would it be a reaction against the rich colouring of French impressionism, the overcoming of which was part of the development of Satie's aesthetics? Or would it be taken more as a joke, as might be suggested by his account of eating nothing but white foods to get into the right mood? Or even as a pun on the French expression 'mariage blanc', referring to a chaste marriage (such as the one of the gay Prince and the lesbian Princess Edmond de Polignac, the latter, as mentioned, being the woman who commissioned from Satie a piece based on Plato's dialogues)? And would the ludic white necessarily oppose the seriousness of classical white?

Every scholar who has written about *Socrate* has found in it some form of whiteness. White is thought of as being articulated in the music's overall homogeneity, in its abundant reiterations; in the lack of contrasts, peaks, or anything that would stand out; in its minimal range of expression and drama; in material that shuns change and development; in a harmonic language that is neither directional nor goal-oriented; in its absence of melody; in its repetitive rhythmic profile; in dynamics that are narrowly defined; in a flat and unadorned vocal delivery. White is the articulation of the work's tininess: '[*Socrate*] is a very tiny world, but it is self-reflected into infinity' (Mellers, 1942, p. 222). A white composition is taken as one that simulates stasis, immobility, a-temporality, and aspires to spatiality and plasticity. It has been suggested that white is a way for Satie to think music's bare essentials. Pietro Dossena, studying the sketches, writes that 'all the variants of *Socrate* have a sort of common denominator, which could be defined—in a very generic way—as the search for restraint and essentiality: the "oscillation range" within which the variants "move" is prescribed within precise limits' (2008, pp. 13–6).

Visual white

A white canvas or a blank page is a prior, as it were, as-yet-untouched place of beginnings, an opening towards an emergence. White is the background or border of what outlines, frames and is excluded. White is a way to flatten out three dimensionalities. It negates colour. To call music white is to think of music in terms of the visual arts. Poulenc makes this explicit when he says that '*Socrate* isn't a fresco of Puvis or of Denis. It is a still life of Picasso. [...] It is the beginning of horizontal music that will follow perpendicular music' (quoted in Orledge,

1990, p. 133). A visual image also lies at the core of the preface Satie requested that René Chalupt write for him:

> This drawing [Satie's *Socrate*], with its precise and strict lines [...], this carefully calibrated and tempered light with no zones of chiaroscuro [...] which never decomposes into impressionist flutterings, this subtle and expert equilibrium of the score engraved on the following pages; it is rather as if M. Ingres, at the request of Victor Cousin, had illustrated these passages from the 'Dialogues of Plato'. Concerning Socrates's spiritual influence, concerning the essence of the Greek soul, the transposition, without pedantism and purely intuitive, which Erik Satie has attempted, brings to us, perhaps, more illumination than weighty works of erudition.
>
> (Satie, 2000, p. 357, quoted in Dayan, 2011, p. 44; preface to Erik Satie, *Socrate* [Paris: Editions de la Sirène, 1919 or 1920])

This is not the only time a comparison with Ingres was suggested. Cocteau opposes Satie's *Gymnopedies* to Debussy's orchestration of it, likening Satie's composition to Ingres's clear smooth line and Debussy's version to Monet's impressionism:

> Hear his '*Gymnopedies*' so clear in their form and melancholy feeling. Debussy orchestrates them, confuses them, and wraps their exquisite architecture in a cloud [...]. The thick lightning-pierced fog of Bayreuth becomes a thin snowy mist flecked with impressionist sunshine. Satie speaks of Ingres; Debussy transposes Claude Monet 'in the Russian style'.
>
> (Cocteau, 1926, pp. 16–7, 33)

Ingres's concern for detail, continuity of line, and smooth contours and curves, as well as his serial self-replications and—most attractive to the cubists—simultaneous viewpoints[17] strike close to Satie's preferred qualities.

Simply white

In his letters from the period of *Socrate*, Satie writes that the work is 'a return to classic simplicity with modern sensibility', adding 'I owe this return—to good uses—to my "cubist" friends'.[18] This passing reference to Cubism is revealing. The composer might have in mind the collaboration with Picasso, Cocteau, and Diaghilev on *Parade*, composed just before *Socrate*. The pairing of whiteness and Cubism might also refer to the tendency of Cubist painting of the period—Picasso's in particular—to do away with colour. Such painting tended towards a grey-brown palette; its construction of the pictorial plane from stereometric forms resulted in a new form of uncoloured painting. This is particularly important if one bears in mind that colour is the medium of harmony in painting. How is one to remain within the space of painting while foregoing a principle of composition based on colour harmony? And what would a principle of composition in music *be* if it were not based on harmony? We will return below to John Cage's response to this question in presenting his understanding of Satie's achievement. It would seem that white, whatever else it is, is identified with simplicity by Satie. The modern sensibility seeks simplicity. That may be more than a formal characterization; it may be something of an existential necessity.

Satie turns against the surfeit of European tradition. Satiated with culture, he wants to compose something that has the limpid clarity of the utterly simple. But is there a way to work towards simplicity, constructively as it were, yet without conforming to the canon or forms of the past? Can there be a kind of art that does not take the form of acting, that is, of making something in particular, but whose plain lightness is truly *entre actes*? Wouldn't this doing away with the making of something that stands out lead to ambient music, to be absorbed in passing? Here is Satie's manifesto-like pronouncements for a Furniture Music:

> Insist upon Furniture Music. Have no meetings, no get togethers, no social affairs of any kind without Furniture Music [...]. Don't get married without Furniture Music. Stay out of houses that don't use Furniture Music. Anyone who hasn't heard Furniture Music has no idea what true happiness is [...]. We must bring about a music which is like furniture, a music, that is, which will be part of the noises of the environment, will take them into consideration [...]. To make such a noise would respond to need.

Furniture music

Indeed, around the time of *Socrate*, the composer first experimented with furniture music. In 1917, early on in the process of composition, Satie devised an outline of the work. He writes it on the hand-copied translation of Plato by Victor Cousin:

The Banquet.- Furniture music.   Frame (dance).
-For a drawing room.   Tapestry (The Banquet, subject).
                                    Frame (dance, repeat).

Phaedrus.-Furniture music.	Colonnade (dance).
-For an entrance hall.	Bas-relief (marble, subject).
	Colonnade (dance, repeat).
Phaedo.- Furniture music.	Casket (hog's hair, dance).
-For a glass display case.	Cameo (Agate of Asia-Phaedo, subject).
	Casket (hog's hair, dance, repeat).[19]

The outline shows three parts corresponding to the three dialogues chosen. Each part is further divided into three (threes are Satie's preferred proportion of division and multiplication, used frequently throughout his career) (Shattuck, 1968, p. 141). Each of the parts is assigned a location ('For a drawing room', 'For an entrance hall', 'For a glass display case'). Some refer to ancient Greek architecture ('colonnade'), others to sculpture ('bas relief').

Each of the parts is in tripartite ABA form, for which the recurring A part is designated 'dance', and the central B section is designated 'subject'. Caroline Potter identifies immobility and whiteness as the main ideas underlying Satie's outline. The dance sections are understood to be static poses, and the materials reference white. Overall, in Potter's view, the structure intones balance and symmetry.[20]

One can argue that the outline might indicate music heard and also composed in response to space. Would it be tied to social function (drawing room, entrance hall), to the material and texture used (tapestry, marble), to labour or sculptural technique, specifically that of carving (bas relief, cameo), or to a means of containment (casket)? It would seem that music not to be listened to differs according to space, and each part in the outline elicits a brand of un-listening. Satie generates rooms, crafts objects, fashions un-listened-to music to match places, purposes and ambience. Music, like light and heat, transpires in space: '"Furniture music" creates vibrations', he writes, 'it has no other aims; it fulfils the role as light, heat and *comfort* in all its forms' (quoted in Potter, 2016, p. 145).

Underlying this notion of music is a game of reversals, deemphasizing music's temporality, overemphasizing architectural motionlessness; as though moving about the listener is immobile sound: 'Before I [Satie] write a piece, I walk around it several times, accompanied by myself'.[21] Music arrested within columns, gouged in stone, as background, ridding itself of any dependency on development or directionality. Is *Socrate* in this mode? And what then would 'hog's hair' refer to? Do we find ourselves here in the context of Dada?

The early outline and its bearing on furniture music is quite enigmatic in light of Satie's final version. This ultimate iteration of the
piece calls for a mode of listening geared to minute detail and nuance,
which requires concentration and attentive listening and is meditative
in quality. Furniture music, by contrast, is designated as background:
One is unaware of it, the music requires no effort and calls for no attention, simulating an unnoticeable silence. And yet the programme
notes of the final composition guide the listener otherwise: 'Those who
are unable to understand are requested by me to observe the most re-
spectful silence and to maintain an attitude of complete submission
and inferiority' (Volta, 1989, p. 155). He wants white listening? Is furniture music an idea that Satie ultimately abandoned? Or can we detect
remnants of this idea in *Socrate*?

Respectful silence

The music of *Socrate* lacks contrasts, high points and a range of dramatic expression. Nothing really stands out, and the music does not really arrive anywhere. There is an insistent suffocation of conventional
musical means—melodic profile, functional harmony, and rhythmic
propulsion. The piece is in conjunct motion, syllabic, and conversa-
tional. The voice line is not organized into motivic groups, patterns,
or tuneful lines. The voice setting is speech-like as if of someone who
is continuously talking, pausing only for breath. No attempt at realism
or lyricism is made in any way. Neither does melodiousness migrate to
the instrumental parts. The orchestra is steady in its unmelodic, short
ostinato figures. These are formulaic, simple, non-developmental, tex-
turally modest, consistent in their rhythmic profile, insistent, monochromatic. Typically, Satie carves his world out of a small amount of
similar music material, constantly reiterated, only slightly varied. In
Socrate these figures are characterized by orchestration: the strings,
for instance, reiterate the figure of the rising scale. These 'sound objects' (see Albright, 2001, pp. 22–39) are not devised in response to text;
rather, they take part in a compositional aesthetic guided by phrasing,
rhythm and timbre.

In the final third part, 'The Death of Socrates', the terms become
sterner. The music material further decreases, more of it is carved out
and removed. There is more repetition, constancy, and confinement.
A single motif, minimally altered and folding into itself. Less and less
music is present, the intervals are narrow. There is an insistence on
unchangeability. Indeed, the work begins in intervals that steadily
contract from one measure to the next, until they arrive on the non-
interval of the prima (see upper voice Music EX 3.1). Satie starts out

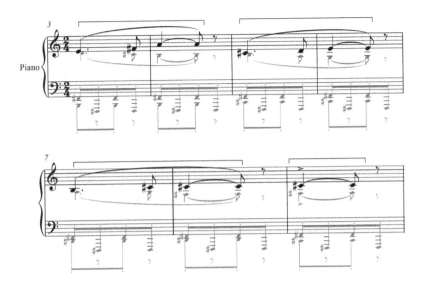

Music Example 3.1 Socrate by Satie mm. 3-9. Paris: Éditions de la Sirène, 1919.

with material whose potential for engendering new material he has already reduced, and then removes more, wishing that the music would lose both depth and surface. It is a reduction to the simplest expression, eliminating everything seemingly extraneous. The composition becomes an exploration of what essentiality entails. The economy is undeniably striking. '*Socrate*', writes Mellers (1987, p. 222), 'is, I think, essentially negative music'; '*Socrate*,' Shattuck (1968, p. 160) writes, 'is that rare phenomenon, utterly *white* music, which denies its own existence as it goes along'.

Restaging *Socrate*

Satie's *Socrate* is exceptional in that it proved inspirational for several important artists in the 20th century. These artists transformed *Socrate* and recast it into their music, sculpture, and painting. It is instructive to view these re-doings and the ways the enigmatic character of Satie's piece is interpreted. Before detailing our staging/interpretation, let us take a look at these attempts to interpret *Socrate*.

In 1944, John Cage wrote a transcription of the first part of Satie's *Socrate* for two pianos to choreography by Merce Cunningham, entitled *Idyllic Song*. When Cunningham returned to Satie's work in 1969 and wished to provide choreography for the two remaining parts,

Satie's publisher denied him the rights to use the music. Cage, calling the work *Cheap Imitation*, retained the rhythmic structure of Satie's phrases, predominantly those of the vocal line, with the pitches being determined by chance. His efforts were directed towards Cunningham's preservation of the choreography.[22] Cunningham, accordingly, gave his reconstruction of the 1944 *Idyllic Song* the title *Second Hand*—which, especially when paired with Cage's compositional practice of imitation, also suggests duplication or something twice removed from its original. The title *Second Hand* is also suggestive of the rule of the small unit of time, the second hand of the clock. What is it to compose with the small, with the unit of seconds in mind? Doesn't experience require breadth, *durée*, as Bergson called it? This turn to smallness is also suggested in Cage's lecture 'Defense of Satie' (1948). Cage contrasts Satie's music with the compositional practices of the past in which meaning is founded on thematic development and on tonality. It is identified in its highest manifestation with Beethoven, the composer of the great, the heroic or the titanic. Cage finds a similar sensibility directed towards the small in Paul Klee:

> It is a great necessity to have to start with the smallest. I want to be as though new-born, knowing nothing, absolutely nothing, about Europe; ignoring poets and fashions, to be almost primitive. Then I want to do something very modest; to work out by myself a tiny formal motive one that my pencil will be able to hold without technique. One favorable moment is enough. The little thing is easily and concisely set down. It's already done! It was a tiny but real affair and someday, through the repetition of such small, but original deeds, there will come one work upon which I can really build.

The minimal whiteness of Satie's work also migrates in an indirect way to Jasper Johns's design for Cunningham's *Second Hand*:

> Second Hand had no décor, and Jasper Johns designed the costumes, each of a single color except for the edge of the arm or leg on one side where another color enters. The second color in each costume was the primary color for another dancer's costume, and as the dancer's bowed, they were arranged in order to show the color succession.

Together the dancers formed a prismatic refraction or rainbow effect. One can see here a refraction of Satie's understanding of whiteness, if one accounts for the fact that white light, according to Newtonian optics, is composed of the distinct colours of the spectrum.

In *Cheap Imitation*, we recognize Cage's novel ideas concerning silence—about music's negative space, what occurs when rhythm rather than harmony governs structure. For Cage, this is equivalent to the negative space in Satie's phrasing. Cage locates Satie's innovation in his rhythmic structure, specifically in the treatment of phrases: Their lengths expand and contract, wax and wane. Satie, unpredictable and non-teleological in treating musical transitions and continuities, employs what Cage terms 'empty structure' (see Perry, 2014). This is an approach to time and sound without expectations that relegates parameters into raw material—call them sonic found objects, or solidly crafted phonic artefacts, or 'objects made of sound, occupying space' (Albright, 2001, p. 26). Cage finds three schematic representations of empty time structure in Satie's work. The first is the symmetrical layout of rhythmic values, which negates any principle of organicism. The second is diatonic and concerns the whole-tone motivic materials; the third is repetition (see Perry, 2014). Cage's treatment of Satie's material reproduces Satie's treatment in exploring the bare, reductionist, skeletal, sculptural form. Whiteness for both these composers is the preoccupation with neutrality and dissociation (Clausius, 2011, pp. 11–2). But in creating his own aesthetic, nothing of what Cage draws on from Satie's aesthetic is related to the text, to Plato or to the portrait of Socrates. In Cage's eyes, this eschewal of the Socratic-Platonic context could also serve as an imitation of what Satie had done.

In 1922, Constantin Brancusi, inspired by Satie's *Socrate*, created three sculptures: *Plato*, *Socrates*, and *Socrates's Cup*. All three are studies of bare essentials: Whiteness, smooth surfaces and the integration of empty space. Hollow space becomes matter and skeletal form. Brancusi integrates the surroundings into these works, dissolving divisions between the work and that which surrounds and lies outside it. The figure's empty cavities articulate negative space, integrating emptiness, the background, into the work. Rosalind Krauss (1986b, p. 283) argues that what emerges is 'a strict opposition between the built and the not-built, the cultural and the natural, between which the production of sculptural art [appears] to be suspended'. Empty space forms the sculpture's matter; hollowness shapes contours; a simple smooth treatment of materials forms the subject matter. Brancusi construes an object out of a principle gesture, a movement, an essence. His process is one of stripping, analogous to Satie's exploration of simplicity and subtraction and his pursuit of abstraction. Brancusi's *Socrates* is suspended 'between form and formal absence' writes Katharina Clausius, 'the sculpture's concentrated, streamlined stance depicts an uncomplicated figure whose most prominent feature is the two holes or negative spaces marking a primitive mouth and cranial cavity. Form here becomes literally skeletal. The philosopher's head, mouth, and eyes (all that characterizes his face) are each outlined against the white gallery wall. Socrates does not have eyes per say but outlines (or absences), which, set against a neutral background, surface more definitely' (Clausius, 2011, p. 16). Krauss classifies such pieces as 'sculpture [that becomes] a kind of ontological absence' (Krauss, 1986b, p. 282). Both Cage and Brancusi see their reflection in Satie: '[T]he interplay between structure and empty space [in Brancusi's *Socrates*] offers a provocatively tangible version of Cage's' (Clausius, 2011, p. 11). In Cage's piece, rhythm, founded on Satie's phrasal pauses, is comparable to the interaction of form and empty space in Brancusi's *Socrates*; silence punctuating sound to produce rhythm and an erect structure is akin to negative space and solid material comprising the figural form. *Socrate* holds an attraction not only within but also outside the worlds of music.

Georges Braque's painting *Socrate: Nature morte a la partition de Satie* is another transposition of Satie's *Socrate*.[23] Braque relegates the renewed interest in antiquity to the context of Cubism, in which *Socrate*'s music is viewed as a Cubist painting:

> Satie discovered in Cubism a similar abhorrence of illusion with its concerted attempt to highlight the two-dimensionality of the painted surface. At the same time, the Cubist creation of a totality through the interlocking of seemingly disjointed pieces was akin to Satie's compositional aesthetic, which relied on a similar internal logic of unrelated sound blocks fused into a synergistic and coherent whole.
>
> (Weiser, 1998, pp. 61–2)

As we have seen, Satie's Cubism is expressed in his treatment of music and in the text—for example, by his selections of three short, non-consecutive excerpts out of the many dialogues featuring Socrates, the cuts he makes, and so on. The technical and aesthetic affinities between Satie and Braque led the visual artist to be attracted to the work of the composer: In the appeals of each to simplicity, collage, juxtaposition and so on, both are cubists (Barbe, 1997, pp. 209–32). The painting *Socrate: Nature morte a la partition de Satie* includes a fragment of the title page of *Socrate*'s score, the composer's name, a stringless guitar and empty staff paper. Peter Dayan (2011) interprets the partial musical instrument, empty staff paper, the fragmented title and the like in *Socrate: Nature morte a la partition de Satie* as exemplifying the art of the period's attraction to music. The mute medium's impossibility of rendering sound is reflected in the portrayal of music as silent: A guitar with no strings, a score with no notes. Braque, like Brancusi and Cage, finds prefigured in Satie's *Socrate* his own aesthetics. Satie's music already embodies the aspiration to a new aesthetics.

In 1936, the composer and critic Virgil Thomson was instrumental in putting together a performance of Satie's *Socrate* at the Wadsworth Atheneum in Hartford, Connecticut, the work's American premiere. The stage design consisted of a mobile designed by the sculptor Alexander Calder, whose invention of a kind of kinetic sculpture—the mobile—in fact resulted from his devising of *Socrate*'s set.[24] A red disk, suspended at centre stage, moved continuously left and right along a horizontal line, complemented by a vertical white rectangle which, tilted to its side, fell flat and rose again on its other, black side to a vertical position. The third element consisted of two steel hoops rotating around a common axis. 'The whole thing was very gentle', Calder writes of these movements, 'and subservient to the music and the words [...] To combine one or two simple movements with different periods, however, really gives the finest effect, because while simple, they are capable of infinite combinations'.[25] This account resonates with Satie's idea that simplicity engenders infinite nuance. While the colours of the set did not suggest whiteness in particular, the gentle movement conveyed the separation of the design from principles of the structuring of space, and from any internal relation to musical or dramatic unfolding. It mirrored the sense of a separation between the planes of the musical and of the dramatic in Satie's work. Virgil Thomson wrote that Calder's set was 'so plain to look at and yet so delicately complex in its movements [...] so rigidly aloof from any over-obvious illustrating of it, that it remains in my memory as one of our century's major achievements in stage investiture'. This emphasis on the relative independence of the musical unfolding and the unfolding of the movement, as though each possesses its own internal logic and runs parallel to the other, is a response to the simplicity of Satie's work. There is no synthesis of image and music or any relation established between their respective realms. Rather, it is as though the movement on stage is self-enclosed yet hovers above the movement of the music, which itself is disconnected from the dramatic quality of the text. This dissociation of music and stage movement was something that Satie had resorted to in composing for René Clair's *Entr'acte*. There, his music was responsive to a problem of synchronization between cinematic image and music. It contained sections that were expandable to allow them to match the end of scenes. But, more importantly, the very possibility of working freely with the dimension of time, without in any way harming the unity of the work, was already a result of Satie's principles of composition. It lies at the centre of how the revolutionary character of his work should be understood.

Voice and music echoed in staging and set

Understanding the abstract[26] quality of *Socrate*, it being about music and specifically about philosophy's complex relationship with the intensity of music, informed the way the performance I directed was conceived.[27] I have described the three musical myths that bring out how Satie is concerned thematically with the power of music. In particular, he addresses the power of the voice and singing to present one of Socrates's main philosophical themes, the immortality of the soul. Satie's work extracts from the Platonic account of the philosopher's life and death myths about the power of music, and the promise of immortality that it harbours. This is implied by the character of the passages he chose from the dialogues, which concern the immortality of music (Marsyas), unending singing (the cicadas) and intimations in song of a prophetic knowledge of one's own death (the swan).

The work of the performers and the design of the set serve to express the three musical myths at the centre of *Socrate*, elaborating the musical meaning extracted from the dialogues, so that staging is distant from the text, not unlike the way the music is divorced from the textual setting.

As mentioned above, Satie left the roles unspecified and fluid. Socrate can be performed by one to four female singers, and this variability, of course, downplays specificity. There is no difference between the philosopher and other figures. The staging accentuated this mutability by casting one singer. The use of a countertenor for all the roles yields floating, unanchored characters. As in my two previous stagings, I am attracted to the countertenor as a disembodied voice. I tapped into the woman's-voice-in-man's-role (in the initial perception of *Socrate*) by casting a man-in-woman's-voice. The aim was to produce a white voice, at least if one goes with the following characterization:

> we might call a white voice, on the analogy of the whiteness of white light or white noise, that [which] include[s] all possible frequencies within them. Such a voice has minimal colour, taste or locative twang; it is, so to speak, *vocality itself*, without the distinguishing grain that would tie it to a particular space, time, or body.
>
> (Connor, 2009, pp. 12–3, emphasis mine)

The singer is positioned predominantly in the dark, gliding onto and off the stage. By destabilizing the stage, the voice determined the borders of the performance event: Set, props, stage business, bodies, everything seemed to be emerging, to be an outcome of voice. Though the text is abundant and comprehensive, signification is derived from the performance of the voice.

The set is minimal and almost unicolour, just as the music is. One singer, one instrument: Clear, symmetrical, transparent props, a dominance of open space. The set consisted of two pairs of transparent glass, aquarium-like receptacles placed on a foundation of concrete blocks. In the first pair, one receptacle is filled with clear water, the other with turbid, milky water; in the second pair, one receptacle is filled with slabs of white wax, and the second is left empty. These gradations of white evoke discolourations of the wine (*Symposium*), the water in the river (*Phaedo*) and poison (*Phaedrus*). The four aquariums divide the stage symmetrically; the different shades, transparent and opaque with respect to their content, ever so slightly affect the symmetry. The change is slight, the receptacles nearly identical, but they are nevertheless variants of one another: The compositional technique—that is, the musical logic—is echoed in the set.

The aquariums are situated on rows of hollow cement building blocks. The grey blocks display tones along the colour spectrum, from transparent, opaque-white, white, grey, to black. Blocks enhance a sense of materiality by enabling the passage of light. The strict colour scheme is founded on diverse materials: Glass, water, wax, honey, paper, wood, plastic, light, hair, fabric, cement. Though a source of light can be white, and light is the medium of vision and is thus in some sense transparent, white in fact is always opaque. This small complication set the tone for the set design's main prop, the aquarium, and its colouration (see Image 3.1).

Satie's compositional technique is often referred to in terms of laboratory trials. The composer is an alchemist experimenting with tiny units as he cuts, stiches, makes incisions, and recombines them. The activity that takes place throughout the performance in relation to these receptacles has the character of small experiments. It involves phenomena such as reflection, the refraction of beams of white light, the change of state from liquid to solid, shadows, light projections achieved through different media, imprints, the dripping of viscous fluids, and capillary action. The experiments produce effects that border on beauty yet are the result of natural processes. They further resonate with central themes from Plato's philosophy, which features shadows, wax, imprints, and reflections among its pre-eminent figures.

Image 3.1 Socrate. The set. Photographer: Eyal Izhar (Performer: Ryo Takenoshita).

On the side of the stage, as part of the set, rests a black grand piano. Lighting alters the silhouettes of the instrument and the instrumentalist. A black draping cloth is spread on the piano's lid and extends down to the floor, creating a stage underneath the lid. From time to time this black hole sucks in the performers. The piano therefore modifies the size of the stage, even though its large dimensions, awkwardness and tuning demands immobility. The piano also modifies the acoustics. When it merges and disappears into the black surroundings, or when it becomes a small stage in and of itself, the sound differs.

Two musical toys, black and white toy grand pianos, lean on the construction blocks, twinned with the grand piano: The latter is large, elegant, sleekly black whereas the former are its diminutive, cheap, odd, white doubles. The toys, miniatures of the stage piano, make up the swan wings in the staging of the third part (see Image 3.2). The

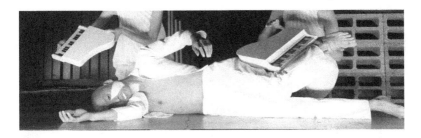

Image 3.2 Socrate. Swan Song. Photographer: Eyal Izhar (Performer: Ryo Takenoshita).

wings, fashioned by pianos, ascend and descend. They glide steadily in a gesture of breath, inhaling and exhaling; it is the mechanism of singing. Wings formed of pianos simulate singing. In commenting on the contest between Marsyas and Apollo, between wind and string instruments, the staging adds the piano and adds singing to the pool of godly paragons.

When death approaches, the toy piano echoes the voice with its clumsy, out-of-tune-plastic-toy timbre. This is an effort to impersonate the singer's voice, an attempt to have the visual collide with the acoustic. As with colour, this is a way to conceive music through other media.

Staging images of music

The first part, the contest between Apollo and Marsyas and their opposed musicianship, is staged via the use of light, movement and textiles. Apollo's lyre is a construction of fluorescent lights, lit progressively, in accordance with the pace of the music. The god's 'trick' of reversing the lyre is figured in the refraction of light in glass and water, suggesting both a scientific experiment and some enchanting, magical phenomenon. This magic of refraction is nevertheless a magic trick, a ruse to subdue the satyr (see Image 3.3).

The satyr's musical instrument is one with his body. That is, I do not use a prop to figure the aulos; rather, the playing is completely embodied in the movement of a performer-dancer. His body contorts and convulses until, upon its ultimate defeat by Apollo, the satyr is immobilized.

There are several ways to distinguish the Apollonian from the Dionysian satyr. The opposition of light and body is the central means

Image 3.3 Socrate. Apollo's lyre of light refracted in glass. Photographer: Eyal Izhar.

of differentiation. But with the representation of the overt struggle of Marsyas against Apollo, my wish was also to suggest, implicitly, Nietzsche's understanding of their coming together. So even though the dancer portrays the satyr and Apollo is portrayed by the other two performers, I had the latter take up, as it were, the emblematic part of Marsyas's body. That which marks a satyr, a hairy tail, is detached, objectified. Long hair, which in colour and texture were aligned with the set's palette, figures as a prop and become a characteristic of the Apollonian performers.

A further challenge occurred in making present the instrument formed by the skin of the flayed Marsyas. The resounding skin was formed by attaching a substantial amount of long black fabric to the black piano. As the Apollonian performers leave the stage, they stretch out the piano's shape with the fabric, reshaping the piano as a huge amorphous wind instrument, inflating and deflating on stage as the pianist is improvising on the final measure.

In the second part, one of the paramount concerns was to bring out the tranquillity of the setting, in which the never-ending song of the cicadas resounds. I created a sense of a rhythm of nature, a serene and harmonious unfolding of natural life, through the unfolding of a shape in the aquariums. Folded paper gradually, as it absorbs the water, unfolds as it sinks into the aquarium. Like Calder's kinetic mobile, the movement seems to be an outgrowth of the music's movement. The unfolding of the paper is perceived as being in complete coordination with the equal-tempered music of Satie, thus creating the scene's sense of tranquil movement.

The never-ending song of the cicadas represents something of the immortality of nature, its partaking in eternal ideas, by having song continually pass away and simultaneously be regenerated. This effect is created by a merging of sounds of multiple individuals into one continuous humming. In staging the movements of the performers in the second part, I foregrounded and visualized what stands in the background of the dialogue: The sounds of the cicadas. So as to present the indiscernibility of the multiple songs of the cicadas, the three performer-dancers formed a conglomerate body that moved ceaselessly, as though producing endless sound (see Image 3.4). Just as the endless sounds of the cicadas' singing are consistent with the short life of the individual insect, so I suggest that the plurality of performers forming one body is intended to be something like a visual analogue of this state.

Image 3.4 Socrate. Cicada formation. Photographer: Eyal Izhar (Performer: Ryo Takenoshita).

Staging Socrates's death

One of the central experiments of the performance was setting Socrates's preparation for death and the process in which the poison works its way through his body and gradually paralyzes him until he dies. How is one to suggest the theme of immortality in presenting the arresting or limit-moment of death itself? By linking visually and thematically the third part to the second, I aimed to draw a parallel between the philosopher's preparation for death, and even his death itself, with the serenity in endless tranquil movement that is felt in and through the unfolding of nature. This connection between two parts of the work is based thematically on material from the dialogues: In the *Phaedrus*, from which the second part is taken, the fundamental repose or restfulness experienced in the beauty of the natural landscape explicitly mirrors the state of the soul before birth as it partakes, so it is said, in the eternal ideas. And the return to that same state, evoked in the *Phaedo*, is what constitutes the third part of Satie's work. Linking the two scenes introduces the endless tranquil movement in nature into Socrates's composed, calm and peaceful death. Such a death is an outcome, indeed the culmination of a life in philosophy. And his preparation for death nowhere betokens tragedy or crisis, as though culmination necessitates an end or a breakdown. Rather, he converses with his disciples and pupils until the last moment, continuing what he always did in life. Dialogue becomes for him something like perpetual motion. Here, too, the ongoing equalized music, the continual delicate alteration of a reiterated motif, extending beyond the arrival of death in the text, may suggest that death is merely a transition to this higher state of the soul, unencumbered by the demands of the body.

As reviewed earlier, Satie includes in the third part Socrates's tale about how swans, sensing the approach of death, sing more beautifully than ever, rejoicing in the prospect of meeting their god. As mentioned, in Plato, Socrates supplements the tale with men's erroneous interpretation of the swan song: Because men fear death, they believe the swans' last sounds to be a lament. Whether the last song is joyous or gloomy, the diverging interpretations depend on the meaning assigned to death. For Socrates, humans hear the song in accordance with the idea they have of it, and the reason for its onset. And yet I ask whether there is not in the sound itself a sense of lament. In staging Satie's musical transposition of philosophy, with his foregrounding of the swan song, I evoke the two interpretations and spur an exploration of how staging alters our understanding of the work. To achieve that duality of meaning, I inserted another swan song: A lament, that echoes what for Socrates, is an erroneous interpretation of the swan song.

Indeed the association of the swan song with lament has attracted a number of composers. Orlando Gibbons's madrigal *The Silver Swan* is one of the best-known examples:

> The silver swan, who living had no note,
> When death approached, unlocked her silent throat;
> Leaning her breast against the reedy shore,
> Thus sung her first and last, and sung no more:
> 'Farewell, all joys; Oh death, come close mine eyes;
> More geese than swans now live, more fools than wise.'

The sorrow is in leaving life behind: 'Farewell, all joys'. Death is unwelcome, and the bird grieves by means of its first, which is also its last, song. *The Silver Swan* is inserted into the third part and performed twice consecutively. It introduces an uncertainty into one's experience of the music, for Renaissance music, Gibbons's 17th-century style, can, for brief bits, sound like Satie. But at the same time it is also clearly different: The scene is in English rather than in French, the language of the opera; it is unaccompanied, whereas the opera contains accompaniment throughout.

The madrigal is performed in a loop. Its staging foregrounds the singer in the act of singing. Rarely is one able to listen to something twice during the same performance. An odd task emerges for the audience: Comparing a singer's performance to itself. The repeated scene exhibits the impossibility of performing and of hearing it identically in both executions. Differences must emerge, even if minute. Indeed, the scene is built so that the tiny differences are introduced in the voice, in singing, so as to stress the 'event' character of singing. Mapping the musical aesthetics onto the performance, the scene works on multiple levels in relation to Satie's composition: On the level of musical procedure, it echoes with Satie's craft of constructing minute musical alterations as it is transported to the performance; on the level of style, it brings out Satie's affinity with early music and tests how far back we can seek some sort of continuity with Satie's music. Moreover, a complementary element is suggested in the form of compensation, as if through Gibbons we include what Satie has left out: The sense of lament in the swan song.

Finally, the creative staging of the scene of the lamenting swan problematizes fundamental assumptions pertaining to the work's relation to its sources and its performances. It asks whether one can introduce instability into Socrates's cheerful acceptance of death, by introducing the interpretation of the swan song as a lament. Did Plato (who pointedly lets us know that he himself was not present) transform the event of Socrates's death in the *Phaedrus*? Did Satie transform Plato's dialogue in setting parts of it to music? Is the performance a transformation of the work as a staging?

The very last scene, the moment of Socrates's transition from life to death, is staged so that it can retain the echo of nature's tranquil rhythm. This time it is produced not by unfolding paper but rather by pouring boiling white wax into the cool water of the aquarium. The wax sinking into the water and gradually solidifying presents, at first, a beautiful landscape of white shapes. But the solidifying of the liquid wax in the aquarium also resonates with the poison infusing Socrates's body and gradually paralyzing him. This change is figured in the solidification of the boiling wax that is gradually poured into an aquarium: Beauty and dread are now unified. The metamorphosis of the living body into a rigid corpse is finally staged by inserting the dancer's hands into the cooled, yet still partly melted wax in the water. The melted wax solidifies around the hands and arms of the performer, immobilizing the movement. In his last gesture the dancer raises his wax-covered arms to hide his face, transforming the mass of rigid wax and body into a death mask (see Image 3.5).

Image 3.5 Socrate. Death scene: Frozen in wax. Photographer: Eyal Izhar (Performer: Ryo Takenoshita).

Notes

1 Pierre Hadot (1995) explains Socratic irony via the way the philosopher's interrogation eventually causes his interlocutors to admit their ignorance and to question their whole life. At the point of crisis in the dialogue, when the interlocutor is discouraged, Socrates takes the failure upon himself and shows the interlocutor the projection of his own self. Socratic irony brings about a movement of consciousness. The interlocutor doesn't learn anything, but he no longer knows anything; through the journey undertaken via the encounter with Socrates, he has experienced the true activity of the mind.

2 The contract with the princess included a piano vocal score. Several of the first performances were with Satie on the piano. It seems the piano vocal score is not only a working score, or is used when an orchestra is unavailable, but is in fact a final version. See below for flexibility also in vocal timbre.

3 For the account regarding Gide see Potter, 2013, pp. 304–5; for the other accounts see Kahan, 2003, pp. 212–3.

4 See Nichols (2002, p. 217).

5 Satie, rather than choose the most important and direct discussion of music in Plato, touches upon music indirectly. He has not selected, for example, a passage like the instance when Plato presents a musical model offered by Socrates's interlocutor, in order to put forth an alternative theory of the duality of soul and body [See 86a–d].

6 See discussion on furniture music below.

7 And not only because cicadas provide a metaphor for the importance of knowing how to detect the difference between philosophy and empty rhetoric.

8 Satie, in effect, positions his listeners in a similar place.

9 Hamilton contrasts Marsyas's position with the model of song sponsored by the Muses and based on inspiration and transmission. The Muses create song by gathering immediate experiences and combining them with what is no longer here: To sing with the Muses is to mourn.

10 Silenus had reared Dionysus. See Wheeler, 1999, pp. 48–9.

11 For elaboration see Hadot, 1995, p. 94.

12 Also included are Socrates's final enigmatic words requesting to sacrifice a rooster and thus repay his debt.

13 Socrates is said to have dreamt, the night before Plato became his student, that a swan flew into his breast.

14 Some believed the sound is caused by the wind blowing through the feathers, others that the swan in fact may be mute.

15 'Has it been noticed that music liberates the spirit? gives wings to thought? that one becomes more of a philosopher the more one becomes a musician?' –Nietzsche, *The Birth of Tragedy*, p. 158.

16 To my knowledge, there is no reference to Nietzsche by Satie. Circuitously, there are connections drawn between the two by Cocteau and Valéry.

17 For example, when anatomical parts in a human portrait, from both the front and the back of the body, are simultaneously in view. Through this comparison, Satie's composition is viewed as a tripartite portrait of Socrates, each part portraying the philosopher from a different

perspective. See Bryson, 1987; Potter, 2016, p. 146; Shattuck, 1968, p. 141, and Weiser, 1998, pp. 41–2, discussed in Krauss, 1986a, pp. 3–7. For Ingres and the Cubists see, for example, Marrinan, 1977.
18 Volta, 1989, p. 152.
19 Reproduced in Potter, 2016, pp. 145–6.
20 Potter, 2016, p. 146.
21 Satie's words in reference to *Apercus desagreables.* In Orledge, 1990, p. 2.
22 *Cheap Imitation* and Satie's *Socrate* preoccupied Cage for a long time. It consists of a series of works spanning many years. Each casts new perspectives distilling further elements in order to draw out a basic idea.
23 Jan Cox's paintings from 1952 and from 1979, *'De dood van Socrates' opgedragen aan Erik Satie*, are other transpositions of Satie's *Socrate* using fragments from the score, text from *Socrate*, the composer's letters and essays, scores from other works and the like.
24 The set was the first time Calder did not use a motor as an external force to create movement. Motion was a direct outcome of a balance between shapes, their weight, and their position in space; in Virgil Thomson's words: 'it was as if the music itself made [Calder's] abstract forms move' (quoted in Volta, 1979, p. 114). See also Bell, 1997.
25 'Mobiles' by Alexander Calder, in Evans, 1937, pp. 62–7. The set was rebuilt by Walter Hatke in 1977 for a reconstructed performance in New York.
26 See Shattuck, 1968, p. 168.
27 TA OPERA ZUTA (2016) performance of *Socrate* at Elma Arts Complex, Zichron Yaakov, Israel, can be seen on my webpage michalgroverfriedlander.com/performances/socrate-satie-2016. **Director:** Michal Grover-Friedlander. **Singer:** Doron Schleifer. **Performers:** Ryo Takenoshita, Noam Sandel, Batel Doten. **Piano:** Daniel Chervinsky. **Set Design:** Eli Friedlander. **Lighting Design:** Iris Mualem. **Producer:** Yoni Garmider. **Costumes:** Michal Grover-Friedlander, Noam Sandel, Mali Aviv. **Set Design Assistants:** Thom Friedlander, Adi Shmulewitz, Shira Yasur.

   Socrate was also performed at Waseda University in Tokyo in collaboration with the Institute for Research in Opera and Music Theatre and the Institute for Advanced Study. I am grateful to the admirable scholars Shizuo Ogino and Arisa Tachi. **Director:** Michal Grover-Friedlander. **Assistant Director:** Mariko Kasahara. **Singers:** Doron Schleifer, Taiki Ikemizu. **Performers:** Ryo Takenoshita, Takehiko Kurokawa, Noam Sandel, Batel Doten. **Piano:** Yuko Yagishita. **Set Design:** Eli Friedlander. **Lighting Design:** Iris Mualem, Yuki Ohnishi. **Stage Manager:** Mao Wada. **Costumes:** Michal Grover-Friedlander, Noam Sandel, Mali Aviv. **Set Design Assistants:** Thom Friedlander, Adi Shmulewitz, Shira Yasur.

References

Abbate, C. (2001) *In search of opera*. Princeton, NJ: Princeton University Press. doi:10.2307/j.ctt1287k8t

Abbate, C. (2004) 'Music–Drastic or gnostic?', *Critical Inquiry*, 30(3), pp. 505–36. doi:10.1086/421160

Albright, D. (2000) *Untwisting the serpent: Modernism in music, literature, and other arts*. Chicago: University of Chicago Press.

Albright, D. (2001) 'Postmodern interpretations of Satie's *Parade*', *Canadian University Music Review / Revue de musique des universités canadiennes*, 22(1), pp. 22–39. doi:10.7202/1014497ar

Albright, D. (2007) *Musicking Shakespeare: A conflict of theatres*. Rochester, NY: University of Rochester Press. doi:10.7722/j.ctt14brrtt

Alston, A. and Welton, M. (eds.) (2017) 'Introduction: The dark draws in', in Alston, A. and Welton, M. (eds.) *Theatre in the dark: Shadow, gloom, and blackout in contemporary theatre*. London: Bloomsbury, pp. 1–34.

Assaf, O. (2010) 'Yes, no ... and possibly: Kurt Weill's music for *The yes sayer*', programme notes for performance of the opera at Tel Aviv University, 2010 [in Hebrew].

Barbe, M. (1997) 'Un aspect de l'humanisme au XX siècle: La convergence des arts (L'example de *Socrate* d'Erik Satie et de la *Nature morte a la partition de Satie* de Georges Braque)', in Guillot, P. and Jambou, L. (eds.) *Histoire, humanisme, et hymnologie: mélanges offerts au professeur Edith Weber*. Paris: Presses de l'Université Paris-Sorbonne, pp. 209–232.

Bell, J. (1997). 'Puppets and performing objects in the twentieth century', *Performing Arts Journal*, 19(2), pp. 29–46.

Benjamin, W. (2003) *Selected writings*, vol. IV, Eiland, H. and Jennings, M. (eds.). Cambridge, MA: Harvard University Press.

Bernhart, W. and Kramer, L. (eds.) (2014) *On voice*. Amsterdam: Rodopi.

Blau, H. (2002) *The dubious spectacle: Extremities of theatre, 1976–2000*. Minneapolis: University of Minnesota Press.

Borwick, S. (1982) 'Weill's and Brecht's theories on music and drama', *Journal of Musicological Research*, 4(1–2), pp. 39–67. doi:10.1080/01411898208574524

Bouissac, P. (1985) *Circus and culture: A semiotic approach*. Lanham, MD: University Press of America.

Brecht, B. (1985) 'He who says yes / He who says no', in Sauerlander, W. (trans.) *The measures taken and other Lehrstücke*. London: Methuen, pp. 6–68.

Bryson, N. (1987) *Tradition and desire: From David to Delacroix*. Cambridge: Cambridge University Press.

Calico, J. (2008) *Brecht at the opera*. Berkeley and Los Angeles: University of California Press. doi:10.1525/9780520942813-004

Campana, A. (2019) '2059: A utopian turning back', *Opera Quarterly*, 35(1–2), pp. 118–29. doi:10.1093/oq/kbz012

Cavarero, A. (2005) *For more than one voice: Toward a philosophy of vocal expression*, trans. P.A. Kottman. Stanford, CA: Stanford University Press.

Chinese fairy tales. Mount Vernon: Peter Pauper Press, 1946/1961.

Chow, R. (2003) *Women and Chinese modernity: The politics of reading between West and East*. Minneapolis: University of Minnesota Press.

Clausius, K. (2011) 'John Cage's "whiteness": "Cheap imitation"', *Tempo*, 65(258), pp. 11–19. doi:10.1017/S0040298211000350

Cocteau, J. (1926) *A call to order: Written between the years 1918 and 1926 and including "Cock and harlequin," "Professional secrets" and other critical essays*, trans. R.H. Myers. New York: Henry Holt.

Connor, S. (2000) *Dumbstruck: A cultural history of ventriloquism*. Oxford: Oxford University Press. doi:10.1093/acprof:oso/9780198184331.001.0001

Connor, S. (2004) 'Windbags and Skinsongs', conference at the University of London. Retrieved from http://stevenconnor.com/windbags.html.

Connor, S. (2009) 'Writing the white voice', lecture at the sound, silence and the arts symposium, Nanyang Technological University, Singapore, 28 February 2009. Retrieved from http://stevenconnor.com/whitevoice.html

Connor, S. (2014) *Beyond words: Sobs, hums, stutters and other vocalizations*. London: Reaktion Books.

Cook, N. (2013) *Beyond the score: Music as performance*. Oxford: Oxford University Press.

Cook, N. and Pettengill, R. (2013) *Taking it to the bridge: Music as performance*. Ann Arbor: University of Michigan Press.

Coutinho, E., Scherer, K.R. and Dibben, N. (2014) 'Singing and emotion', in Welch, G.F., Howard, D.M. and Nix, J. (eds.) *The Oxford handbook of singing* (online publication). doi:10.1093/oxfordhb/9780199660773.013.006

Cucullu, L. (2009) 'Sleep deprived and ultramodern: How novels turned dream girls into insomniacs', *Novel: A Forum on Fiction*, 42(2), pp. 304–10. doi:10.1215/00295132-2009-019

Dayan, P. (2011) *Art as music, music as poetry, poetry as art, from Whistler to Stravinsky and beyond*. Farnham: Ashgate. doi:10.4324/9781315567969

DeMarco, L.E. (2002) 'The fact of the castrato and the myth of the countertenor', *Musical Quarterly*, 86(1), pp. 174–85. doi:10.1093/musqtl/gdg006

Dolar, M. (2006) *A voice and nothing more*. Cambridge, MA: MIT Press.

Dossena, P. (2008) 'À la recherche du vrai Socrate', *Journal of the Royal Musical Association*, 133(1), pp. 1–131. doi:10.1093/jrma/fkm013

Drew, D. (1965) 'Weill's school opera', *Musical Times*, 106(1474), pp. 934–7. doi:10.2307/954340

Drew, D. (1987) *Kurt Weill: A handbook*. Berkeley and Los Angeles: University of California Press, pp. 226–9.

Ebrey, P.B. (2003) *Women and the family in chinese history*. London: Routledge. doi:10.4324/9780203218211

Eidsheim, N.S. (2009) 'Synthesizing race: Towards an analysis of the performativity of vocal timbre', *TRANS-Transcultural Music Review*, 13(7). Available at https://www.sibetrans.com/trans/articulo/57/synthesizing-race-towards-an-analysis-of-the-performativity-of-vocal-timbre

Eidsheim, N.S. (2015) *Sensing sound: Singing and listening as vibrational practice*. Durham, NC: Duke University Press.

Eidshem, N.S. and Meizel, K. (eds.) (2019) *The Oxford handbook of voice studies*. Oxford: Oxford University Press.

Espiner, T. and Home-Cook, G. in interview with Alston, A. and Welton, M. (2017) 'Darkness, perceptual ambiguity and the abyss', in Alston, A. and Welton, M. (eds.) *Theatre in the dark: Shadow, gloom, and blackout in contemporary theatre*. London: Bloomsbury, pp. 131–46. doi:10.5040/9781474251211

Evans, M. (ed.) (1937) *The painter's object*. London: Gerold Howe.

Feldman, M. (2015a) *The castrato: Reflections on natures and kinds* (Ernest Bloch lectures). Oakland: University of California Press. doi:10.1525/j.ctt13x1hwq

Feldman, M. (2015b) '"An interstitial voice: An opening"', colloquy 'Why voice now', *JAMS*, 68(3), pp. 653–9. doi:10.1525/jams.2015.68.3.653

Feldman, M. and Zeitlin, J.T. (eds.) (2019) *The Voice as Something More: Essays Toward Materiality*. Chicago: Chicago University Press.

Feurzeig, L. (1997) 'Heroines in perversity: Marie Schmith, animal magnetism, and the Schubert circle', *19th-Century Music*, 21(2), pp. 223–43. doi:10.2307/746899

Ficarra, E. (1995) *The empress's feet*. London: Contemporary Voices, c/o British Music Information Centre.

Ficarra, E. (2017). 'Evelyn Ficarra, about' [online]. Retrieved from https://www.evelynficarra.net/about/. Accessed 11 October 2020.

Fiebach, J. (2005) 'A German's reading of Brecht in 2004: Gestus, dialectic, productivity', in Keynar, G. and Ben-Zvi, L. (eds.) *Bertolt Brecht: Performance and philosophy*. Tel Aviv: Assaph Book Series, pp. 53–68.

Fischer-Lichte, E. (2004) *Ästhetik des Performativen*. Frankfurt am Main: Suhrkamp.

Friedlander, E. (2005) 'Gesture: Benjamin and Brecht', in Keynar, G. and Ben-Zvi, L. (eds.) *Bertolt Brecht: Performance and philosophy*. Tel Aviv: Assaph Book Series, pp. 23–34.

Friedlander, E. and Grover-Friedlander, M. (2012). 'Setting the stage, staging the voice: On directing Weill and Brecht's *Der Jasager*', *Qui Parle: Critical Humanities and Social Sciences*, 21, pp. 203–34.

Frith, S. (2008) 'The voice as a musical instrument', in Clayton, M. (ed.) *Music words and voice: A reader*. Manchester: The Open University, pp. 65–71.

Fugate, B.K. (2016) 'The contemporary countertenor in context: Vocal production, gender/sexuality, and reception', PhD diss., Boston University.

Gautier, A.M.O. (2014) *Aurality: Listening and knowledge in nineteenth-century Colombia*. Durham, NC: Duke University Press.

Gillmor, A.M. (1988) *Erik Satie*. Boston, MA: Twayne.

Gordon, B. (2015) 'It's not about the cut: The castrato's instrumentalized song', *New Literary History*, 46(4), pp. 647–67. doi:10.1353/nlh.2015.0042

Grover-Friedlander, M. (2005) *Vocal apparitions: The attraction of cinema to opera*. Princeton, NJ: Princeton University Press.

Grover-Friedlander, M. (2011a) *Operatic afterlives*. New York: Zone Books.

Grover-Friedlander, M. (2011b) 'Prompting voice in opera', *Opera Quarterly*, 27(4), pp. 460–80. doi:10.1093/oq/kbs033

Grover-Friedlander, M. (2014a) 'Transformations of a killing of a boy: Weill's and Brecht's *Der Jasager*', in Lichtenstein, S. (ed.) *Opera's obedient daughter*. Amsterdam: Rodopi, Textxet series, pp. 381–404. doi:10.1163/9789401210553_016

Grover-Friedlander, M. (2014b) 'Voice', in Greenwald, H. (ed.) *Oxford handbook of opera*. Oxford: Oxford University Press, pp. 318–33.

Grover-Friedlander, M. (2021) 'Voice and the sleeping body', *Theatre Research International*, 46(2), pp. 128–147. doi:10.1017/S0307883321000067

Gumbrecht, H.U. (2005) 'Production of presence, interspersed with absence: A modernist view on music, libretti, and staging', in Berger, K. and Newcomb, A. (eds.) *Music and the aesthetics of modernity*. Cambridge, MA: Harvard University Press, pp. 343–55.

Hadot, P. (1995) *Philosophy as a way of life: Spiritual exercises from Socrates to Foucault*. London: Blackwell.

Hamilton, J. (2013) *Music, madness and the unworking of language*. New York: Columbia University Press. doi:10.7312/hami14220

Hanegraaff, W.J. (2010) 'Magnetic gnosis: Somnambulism and the quest for absolute knowledge', in Kilcher, A.B. and Theisohn, P. (eds.) *Die Enzyklopädik der Esoterik: Allwissenheitsmythen und universalwissenschaftliche Modelle in der Esoterik der Neuzeit* Paderborn: Wilhelm Fink, pp. 118–134.

Hanna, V. (2015) 'The Aleph-bet song: Official video'. Retrieved from https://www.youtube.com/watch?v–Bl1epz3tSSA.

Harden, S.C. (1972) 'The music for the stage collaboration of Weill and Brecht', PhD diss., University of North Carolina at Chapel Hill.

Heller, W. (2005) 'Varieties of masculinity: Trajectories of the castrato from the seventeenth century', *British Journal for Eighteenth-Century Studies*, 28, pp. 307–21. doi:10.1111/j.1754-0208.2005.tb00304.x

Hennessey, A. and Harnisch, B. (2019) 'Chop-era: The operatic history and modern relevance of the "Castrato"', *Journal of Urology*, 201(4S), supplement, 3 May, p. e246. doi:10.1097/01.JU.0000555400.02067.c0

Hinton, S. (1994) 'Lehrstück: An aesthetics of performance', in Gilliam, B. (ed.) *Music and performance during the Weimar Republic*. Cambridge: Cambridge University Press, 1994, pp. 59–73.

Humphreys, P. (1988) 'Expressions of Einverständnis: Musical structure and affective content in Kurt Weill's Score for *Der Jasager*', PhD diss., University of California, Los Angeles.

Jameson, F. (1998) *Brecht and method.* London: Verso.

Jankélévitch, V. (2003) *Music and the ineffable*, trans. C. Abbate. Princeton, NJ: Princeton University Press.

Kahan, S. (2003) *Music's modern muse: A life of Winnaretta Singer, princesse de Polignac.* Rochester: University of Rochester Press, 2003.

Kalb, J. (1995) 'The Horatian: Building the better Lehrstück', *New German Critique*, 64, pp. 161–73. doi:10.2307/488468

Kane, B. (2015) 'Sound studies without auditory culture: A critique of the ontological turn', *Sound Studies: An Interdisciplinary Journal*, 1, pp. 2–21. doi:10.1080/20551940.2015.1079063

Keene, D. (ed.) (1970) *Twenty plays of the Nō theatre.* New York: Columbia University Press.

Kemp, I. (1993) '*Der Jasager*: Weill's composition lesson', in Kowalke, K. and Edler, H. (eds.) *A stranger here myself: Kurt Weill Studien.* Hildesheim: Georg Olms Verlag, pp. 143–57.

Kendrick, L. (2017) 'Aural visions: Sonic spectatorship in the dark', in Alston, A. and Welton, M. (eds.) *Theatre in the dark: Shadow, gloom, and blackout in contemporary theatre.* London: Bloomsbury, pp. 113–30.

Klaic, D. (1994) 'Restaging Europe New opera: Less is more', *Theater*, 25(1), pp. 72–7. doi:10.1215/01610775-25-1-72

Ko, D. (2005) *Cinderella's sisters: A revisionist history of footbinding.* Berkeley and Los Angeles: University of California Press. doi:10.1525/j.cttlppvlt

Koestenbaum, W. (1993) *The queen's throat: Opera, homosexuality, and the mystery of desire.* New York: Poseidon.

Kolesch, D. (2013) 'Staging voices', *Journal of Contemporary Drama in English*, 1(1), pp. 103–12. doi:10.1515/jcde-2013-0010

Kowalke, K. (1977) *Kurt Weill in Europe, 1900–1935: A study of his music and writings.* New Haven, CT: Yale University Press.

Kowalke, K. (ed.) (1986) *A new Orpheus: Essays on Kurt Weill.* New Haven, CT: Yale University Press.

Kowalke, K. (1993) 'Singing Brecht vs. Brecht singing: Performance in theory and practice', *Cambridge Opera Journal*, 5(1), pp. 55–78. doi:10.1017/S0954586700003888

Kramer, L. (2011) *Interpreting music.* Berkeley and Los Angeles: University of California Press. doi:10.1525/j.cttlpnchw

Kramer, L. (2014a) 'Meaning', in Greenwald, H. (ed.) *The Oxford handbook of opera.* Oxford: Oxford University Press, pp. 353–6.

Kramer, L. (2014b) 'On voice: An introduction', in Bernhart, W. and Kramer, L. (eds.) *On voice.* Amsterdam: Rodopi, pp. vii–xv.

Krauss, R. (1986a) 'The future of an illusion', *AA Files*, 13, pp. 3–7.

Krauss, R. (1986b) *The originality of the avant-garde and other modernist myths.* Cambridge, MA: Harvard University Press.

Kristeva, J. (1986/1991 [1974]) *About Chinese women.* New York: Boyars.

La Cenerentola (1981). Directed by Jean-Pierre Ponnelle [film of Rossini opera]. The singers are Francisco Araiza, Claudio Desderi, Paolo Montarsolo, Margherita Guglielmi, Laura Zannini, and Frederica von Stade.

Claudio Abbado, conductor. Sextet Retrieved from https://www.youtube.com/watch?v–fsNAgFyPAqg. Accessed 11 October 2020.

Levin, D. (2007) *Unsettling opera: Staging Mozart, Verdi, Wagner, and Zemlinsky*. Chicago: University of Chicago Press.

Mabry, S. (2002) *Exploring twentieth-century vocal music: A practical guide to innovations in performance and repertoire*. Oxford: Oxford University Press.

Macpherson, B. (2015) 'Body musicality': The visual, virtual, visceral voice', in Thomaidis K. and Macpherson, B. (eds.) *Voice studies: Critical approaches to process, performance and experience*. New York: Routledge Voice Studies, pp. 149–61.

Macpherson, B. (2021) 'The somaesthetic in-between: Six statements on vocality, listening and embodiment', in Kapadocha, Ch. (ed.) *Somatic voices in performance research and beyond*. New York: Routledge Voice Studies, pp. 212–26.

Madhaven A. and Nair, S. (2013) 'Foot, memory and dispositions of the body in performance', in Reeve, S. (ed.) *Ways of being a body: Body and performance*. Charmouth: Triarchy Press, pp. 149–62.

Malone, J. (1988) '"Let the punishment fit the crime": The vocal choreography of Cholly Atkins', *Dance Research Journal*, 20(1), pp. 11–8. doi:10.2307/1478812

Marrinan, M. (1977) 'Picasso as an "Ingres" Young Cubist', *Burlington Magazine*, 119(896), special issue devoted to European art since 1890, pp. 756, 758–63.

Meizel, K. (2020) *Multivocality: Singing on the borders of identity*. New York: Oxford University Press. doi:10.1093/oso/9780190621469.001.0001

Mellers, W. (1942) 'Erik Satie and the "problem" of contemporary music', *Music and Letters*, 23(3), 210–27.

Mellers, W. (1987) *The masks of Orpheus: Seven stages in the story of European music*. Manchester: Manchester University Press.

Michalgroverfriedlander.com

Mister Golightly (2017) 'Who sang the "Queen of The Night" staccatos the best? (F6)'. Retrieved from https://www.youtube.com/watch?v-KNYws1P-NCH8. Accessed 11 October 2020.

Morley, M. (1986) '"Suiting the action to the word": Some observations on gestus and Gestische Musik', in Kowalke, K. (ed.) *A New Orpheus: Essays on Kurt Weill*. New Haven, CT: Yale University Press, pp. 183–201.

Nacht, J. (1915) 'The symbolism of the shoe with special reference to Jewish sources', *Jewish Quarterly Review*, 6(1), pp. 1–22. doi:10.2307/1451461

Nancy, J.-L. (2007) *Listening*. New York: Fordham University Press.

Neumark, N., Gibson, R. and van Leeuwen, T. (eds.) (2010) *Voice: Vocal aesthetics in digital arts and media*. Cambridge, MA: MIT Press.

Nichols, R. (2002) *The harlequin years: Music in Paris 1917–1929*. London: Thames and Hudson.

Nietzsche, F. (1967) *The birth of tragedy and the case of Wagner*, trans. Walter Kaufmann. New York: Vintage.

Novak, J. (2015) *Postopera: Reinventing the voice-body*. London: Ashgate.

OK Go (2102) '"Needing/Getting": Official video'. Retrieved from https://youtu.be/MejbOFk7H6c.

Orledge, R. (1990) *Satie the composer.* Cambridge: Cambridge University Press.

Parker, R. (2006) *Remaking the song: Operatic visions and revisions from Handel to Berio.* Chicago: University of Chicago Press. doi:10.1525/j.cttlppxhg

Pavis, P. (1982) *Languages of the stage: Essays in the semiology of theatre.* New York: Performing Arts Journal Publications.

Pavis, P. (2013) *Contemporary mise en scène: Staging theatre today.* London: Routledge.

Perry, J. (2014) '"A quiet corner where we can talk": Cage's Satie, 1948–1958', *Contemporary Music Review,* 33(5–6), pp. 483–511. doi:10.1080/07494467.2014.998415

Phelan, P. (1993) *Unmarked: The politics of performance.* Abingdon: Routledge. doi:10.4324/9780203359433

Potter C. (ed.) (2013) *Erik Satie: Music, art and literature.* London: Ashgate, pp. 304–5. doi:10.4324/9781315580180

Potter, C. (2016) *Erik Satie: A Parisian composer and his world.* Woodbridge: Boydell Press. doi:10.7722/j.ctt18gzfkq

Protz, U. (2015) 'Review of Feldman, M., *The Castrato: Reflections on Natures and Kinds', Cultural History,* 5(1), pp. 103–5.

Retallack, J. (ed.) (1996) *Musicage: Cage muses on word, art, music.* Hanover, NH: Wesleyan University Press.

Risi, C. (2006) 'Opera and performance: About voices and bodies and their perception', lecture at the 3rd Annual German-American Frontiers of Humanities Symposium (GAFOH), sponsored by the Alexander von Humboldt Foundation (AvH) and the U.S. American Philosophical Society (APS): 'The making of memory: Space performance appropriation', Philadelphia.

Ritchey, M. (2010) 'Echoes of the guillotine: Berlioz and the French fantastic', *19th-Century Music,* 3–4(2), pp. 168–85. doi:10.1525/ncm.2010.34.2.168.

Rockwell, J. (1986) 'Kurt Weill's operatic reform and its context', in Kowalke, K. (ed.) *A new Orpheus: Essays on Kurt Weill.* New Haven, CT: Yale University Press, pp. 51–9.

Roesner, D. (2014) *Musicality in theatre: Music as model, method and metaphor in theatre-making.* Farnham: Ashgate. doi:10.4324/9781315597003

Satie, E. (2000) *Correspondance presque complète,* ed. O. Volta. Paris: Fayard.

Schneider, R. (2001) 'Performance Remains', *Performance Research,* 6(2), pp. 100–108. doi:10.1080/13528165.2001.10871792

Schelling, F.W.J. (2000) *The ages of the world, third version* (c. 1815), trans. Jason Wirth. Albany: State University of New York Press.

Seibert, B. (2019) 'Cholly Atkins taught Motown to dance. His moves get an update in "Ain't Too Proud"', *New York Times,* March 13.

Shattuck, R. (1968) *The banquet years: The origins of the avant-garde in France – 1885 to World War I.* New York: Vintage.

Sheppard, A. (2001) *Revealing masks: Exotic influences and ritualized performance in modernist music theater.* Berkeley and Los Angeles: University of California Press. doi:10.1525/california/9780520223028.001.0001

Stiles, A., Finger S. and Bulevich, J. (2010) 'Somnambulism and trance states in the works of John William Polidori, author of *The Vampyre*', *European Romantic Review*, 21(6), pp. 794–6. doi:10.1080/10509585.2010.514510

TA OPERA ZUTA. See productions on my webpage michalgroverfriedlander.com

TA OPERA ZUTA (2011) Performance of *Der Jasager*, Tmuna Theatre, Tel Aviv, Israel. michalgroverfriedlander.com/performances/theyessayer-weill-brecht-2011. **Director:** Michal Grover-Friedlander. **Stage Design:** Eli Friedlander. **Masks:** Eli Friedlander, Ofri Omer. **Lighting Design:** Iris Mualem. **Costumes:** Meital Gueta, Moran Sanderovich. **Make Up:** Miri Shamash. **Translation and Text Setting:** Yaniv Baruh. **Conductor:** Bar Avni. **Performers:** Teacher: Doron Schleifer. Child: Yeela Avital. Mother: David Feldman. Doubles: Anat Czarny, Jonahan Opinya. Acrobat: Reenat Caidar Avraham. Students: Efrat Raz, Kfir Levy, Hemi Levinson, Jonathan Opinya. Chorus: Tal Bergman, Maayan Goldenfeld, Shahar Lavi, Hanna Bardos, Noa Hegesh, Haggai Grady, Yoav Weiss, Pavel Pivnev. Piano: Yevgeny Yontov. Flute: Avner Geiger. Clarinet: Hila Zamir. Saxophone: Orr Guy. Violin: Tamar Koren, Daniel Ratush. Cello: Ben Shibolet, Daniel Mitnitsky. Double Bass: Or Shemesh. Guitar: Nimrod Gilboa. Percussion: Almog Turner. **Correpetition:** Yaniv Baruh. **Production:** Michal Grover- Friedlander, Yaniv Baruh, Noa Hegesh.

TA OPERA ZUTA (2014) Performance of *The Empress's feet*, Tmuna Theatre, Tel Aviv. michalgroverfriedlander.com/performances/theempresssfeet-ficarra-whittington-2014. **Singing (recording):** Doron Schleifer. **Performance Artists:** Jonathan Opinya, Ofri Omer, Gony Paz, Reenat Caidar Avraham. **Directing and Artistic Management:** Michal Grover-Friedlander. **Stage Design and Props:** Eli Friedlander, Thom Friedlander, Coline Faucon. **Lighting and Sound Design:** Nadav Barnea. **Production:** Shira Yasur.

TA OPERA ZUTA (2016) Performance of *Socrate*, Elma Arts Complex, Zichron Yaakov. See production on my webpage michalgroverfriedlander.com/performances/socrate-satie-2016. **Director:** Michal Grover-Friedlander. **Singer:** Doron Schleifer. **Performers:** Ryo Takenoshita, Noam Sandel, Batel Doten. **Piano:** Daniel Chervinsky. **Set Design:** Eli Friedlander. **Lighting Design:** Iris Mualem. **Producer:** Yoni Garmider. **Costumes:** Michal Grover-Friedlander, Noam Sandel, Mali Aviv. **Set Design Assistants:** Thom Friedlander, Adi Shmulewitz, Shira Yasur.

Socrate was also performed at Waseda University in Tokyo in collaboration with the Institute for Research in Opera and Music Theatre and the Institute for Advanced Study. I am grateful to the admirable scholars Shizuo Ogino, and Arisa Tachi. **Director:** Michal Grover-Friedlander. **Assistant Director:**

Mariko Kasahara. **Singers:** Doron Schleifer, Taiki Ikemizu. **Performers:** Ryo Takenoshita, Takehiko Kurokawa, Noam Sandel, Batel Doten. **Piano:** Yuko Yagishita. **Set Design:** Eli Friedlander. **Lighting Design:** Iris Mualem, Yuki Ohnishi. **Stage Manager:** Mao Wada. **Costumes:** Michal Grover-Friedlander, Noam Sandel, Mali Aviv. **Set Design Assistants:** Thom Friedlander, Adi Shmulewitz, Shira Yasur.

Tatlow, A. (1977) *The mask of evil: Brecht's response to the poetry, theatre and thought of China and Japan: A comparative and critical evaluation*. Peter Lang: Bern.

Tauber, Z. (2010) 'Two lectures on Brecht's *The yes sayer* and *The no sayer*', programme notes for performance of the opera at Tel Aviv University, 2010 [in Hebrew].

Thomaidis, K. (2020) 'Dramaturging the I-voicer in *A voice is. A voice has. A voice does.*: Methodologies of autobiophony', *Journal of Interdisciplinary Voice Studies*, 5(1), pp. 81–106. doi:10.1386/jivs_00017_1

Thomaidis, K. (2021) 'Foreword: A phonotechnics of vocal somaticity: An autobiophonic note', in Kapadocha, C. (ed.) *Somatic voices in performance research and beyond*. Abingdon: Routledge, pp. xxi–xxvii. doi:10.4324/9780429433030

Thomaidis, K. and Macpherson, B. (eds.) (2015) *Voice studies: Critical approaches to process, performance and experience*. New York: Routledge.

Thomas, S.S. (1995) '"Cinderella" and the phallic foot: The symbolic significance of the tale's slipper motif', *Southern Folklore*, 52(1), pp. 19–31.

Till, N. (2013) 'Stefano Gervasoni's *Pas si*: Staging a music theatre work based on a text by Samuel Beckett', *Contemporary Theatre Review*, 23(2), pp. 220–32. doi:10.1080/10486801.2013.777058

Tsubaki, A. (1995) 'Brecht's encounter with Mei-Lan-Fang (Peking Opera actor) and *Taniko* (Japanese No play)', in Lyon, J. and Breuer, H.-P. (eds.) *Brecht unbound: Presented at the International Bertolt Brecht Symposium held at the University of Delaware, February 1992*. Newark, DE, pp. 163–4.

Vass-Rhee, F. (2010) 'Auditory turn: William Forsythe's vocal choreography', *Dance Chronicle*, 33(3), pp. 388–413. doi:10.1080/01472526.2010.517495

Volta, O. (1979) *L'Ymagier d'Erik Satie*. Paris: Van de Velde.

Volta, O. (1989) *Satie, seen through his letters*, trans. M. Bullock. London: Marion Boyars.

Waley, A. (1957) *The Nō Plays of Japan* [1921]. New York: Grove Press.

Weiser, D.E. (1998) 'The visual stimulus: The influence of the visual arts on the musical compositions of Emmanuel Chabrier, Erik Satie, and Francis Poulenc', PhD diss., Peabody Conservatory of Music, Johns Hopkins University.

Wheeler, S. (1999) *A discourse of wonders: Audience and performance in Ovid's Metamorphoses*. Philadelphia: University of Pennsylvania Press.

Whittington, V. (2020) Faculty home page, University of Essex. Retrieved from https://profiles.sussex.ac.uk/p70284-valerie-whittington. Accessed 11 October 2020.

Wilkins, N. and Satie, E. (1980) 'Erik Satie's letters to Milhaud and others', *Musical Quarterly*, 66(3), pp. 404–28. doi:10.1093/mq/LXVI.3.404

Willett, J. (ed.) (1966) *Brecht on theatre: The development of an aesthetic*, trans. J. Willett. London: Methuen.

Wirth, A. (1971) 'Brecht and the Asiatic model: The secularization of magical rites', *Literature East and West*, 15(4), pp. 601–15.

Index

128   *Index*